INTERESTING WAYS TO TEACH

53 Interesting activities for
for
open learning courses

53 Interesting activities for open learning courses

David Kember

Hong Kong Polytechnic

David Murphy

Deakin University, Australia

First published in 1994 by

Technical and Educational Services Ltd
37 Ravenswood Road
Bristol BS6 6BW
Avon
UK

ISBN 0 947885 85 4

Printed by The Cromwell Press. Broughton Gifford, Melksham, Wilts. U.K.

Books available from Technical and Educational Services Ltd

The 53 series
53 Interesting things to do In your lectures
53 Interesting things to do in your seminars and tutorials
53 Interesting ways to assess your students
53 Interesting ways of helping your students to study
53 Interesting communication exercises for science students
53 Interesting ways to appraise your teaching
53 Interesting ways to promote equal opportunities in education
53 Interesting ways to write open learning material
53 Interesting activities for open learning courses
53 Problems with large classes: *making the best of a bad job*
53 Interesting ways to teach mathematics

Interesting Ways To Teach
Preparing to teach: *An introduction to effective teaching in higher education*
253 Ideas for your teaching
Interesting ways to teach: *Do-it-yourself Training Exercises*
Creating a teaching profile

Other titles
Getting the most from your data: *Practical ideas on how to analyse qualitative data*
Writing study guides
Improving the quality of student learning
HMA Stationery Ltd. *(An open & flexible learning study pack.)*

TES Books are distributed by
Plymbridge Distributors Ltd, Estover, Plymouth PL6 7PZ, Devon, U.K.
For Customer Services telephone 0752.695745 or fax 0752.695699

Acknowledgement of extracts

This book contains numerous extracts from open learning courses to illustrate the principles we discuss and to give you ideas for devising activities of your own. We are grateful to the copyright holders acknowledged below for permission to include these extracts.

The course from which each extract is taken is indicated in the footnote which appears at the end of the Activity.

Extracts

Extracts are shown as in this example with 'brackets' above and below. The extracts are indented from the normal margins. The font is also changed to Helvetica, as used here.

The typographical format of extracts has been altered to provide a consistent style within this book. Some of the extracts have been shortened or simplified to highlight the principle being illustrated.

Extracts for Activities 1, 4, 7, 9, 14, 15, 27, 32, 35 and 37 are Copyright Deakin University 1991/92. They are taken from courses offered by Deakin's Faculty of Education and the Centre for Management Services.

Extracts for Activities 6, 10, 11, 12, 19, 21, 24, 25, 26, 28, 41, 47, 5 and 52 are from courses in the Programme Development Series of the

Hong Kong Polytechnic.

Activity 31 includes an extract taken from the subject Intermediate Pascal offered by the Department of Mathematics and Computing, University of Central Queensland. It is reproduced with the permission of the University of Central Queensland.

Activities 12, 13, 18, 21, 22, 23, 31, 38, 42, 43 and 50 are taken from courses in the Extended-Campus Studies programs of the University of Tasmania at Launceston and appear by permission of the University of Tasmania at Launceston. The courses from which extracts are taken were published in the period 1982 to 1985. Some of these courses have subsequently been superseded or updated so the extracts may not be from the current versions of courses. Nevertheless they illustrate well the principles intended.

The extract in Activity 2 appears with permission of the Association of Professional Engineers and Scientists of Australia.

Extracts in Activities 4 and 30 appear with permission of the Australian Society of Certified Practising Accountants.

Monash University, Australia, has given permission for the extracts used in Activity 16.

Activity 3 contains an extract reproduced with the permission of the National Examining Board for Supervisory Management, London.

The Open Learning Institute of Hong Kong has given permission for the extract which appears in Activity 39.

Extracts in Activities 5 and 40 are taken from *Polymaths book C: Sets, concepts and relations* and appear by permission of a member of the Polymaths course team.

Extracts in Activities 30, 46 and 48 are reproduced with permission of the Distance Education Program, Continuing Education Division University of Manitoba, Canada. In particular, we thank the authors, Professor Lance Roberts of the Department of Sociology and Professor Christina Gow of the Community Health Nursing program.

Extracts in Activities 5 and 33 are taken from the Matriculation Studies Science course of the University of Papua New Guinea and appear by permission of the University of Papua New Guinea.

Activities 8, 34 and 53 contain extracts from courses produced by the University of the South Pacific and appear by permission of Extension Services at the University of the South Pacific.

Special thanks are due to the staff and friends of TES Ltd

who helped in the final production of this book. They are:

John Davidson

Stephen Gomez

Trevor Habeshaw

Dave Lush

Jenny Walters

Contents

Part A Activities in self-instructional packages

Chapter 4   Learning from teaching resources

Part B   Activities in group meetings

Part A

Activities in self-instructional packages

General considerations

An important distinguishing feature between self-instructional packages and text books is the activities. Activities can transform a book from a presentation of content into a tutorial in print. They turn the student from a passive receiver into an active participant and can simulate a dialogue between tutor and student. They thus play a major role in developing quality open learning materials.

Yet, from our experience as instructional designers helping others to develop self-instructional packages, the activities seem to be the hardest part to write. Many writers can develop lucid, well organised lecture notes, handouts or even text books, but seem stuck for ideas when it comes to the activities.

What definitely seems to help is a collection of examples, and this has led to the production of this book, which contains a wide variety of examples from many sources. The book is an organised and categorised version of more chaotic collections of photocopies and study packages the authors have used in the past.

Applicability

The discussion in this book refers to open learning courses and the examples are taken from open learning courses. There is, though, very little which is exclusive to open learning. Most of the educational rationale given in the initial discussion of each activity applies to other forms of education.

Most of the activities could be used equally well in conventional face-to-face teaching. The activities could be set as exercises to be completed in tutorials or seminars. They could also be set as homework for discussion at the next meeting. Many of the activities are particularly suitable for use in structured lectures.

Most of the examples included here have their origins in print-based materials. This is partly because the large majority of open learning courses are print-based, and partly because print is the easiest medium to reproduce in a book. Some could easily be used or modified for use with other media such as audio tapes or computer-based learning.

Answers

Another feature of activities is that, for most courses, feedback is provided within the learning materials. We strongly support this idea, which makes good educational sense.

The feedback can take a variety of forms, depending on the nature of the activity. For those which concern simple recall or straightforward application, definitive answers can be given. More reflective activities obviously require a different style of feedback, with emphasis on the process that the student may have followed and a broad indication of possible arguments or pathways that might have been used.

For most activities we would recommend that the feedback be given at the end of a topic, chapter or unit. The flow of text is not disturbed by this format. Also, students then need to make a conscious action to compare their response to the recommended one. They cannot just look straight at an answer. An exception to this recommendation occurs when the aim is to stimulate a dialogue between writer and student (see Activities 12 to 14). In such cases the feedback or comment is better included immediately after the question.

For most of the extracts given in this book answers to the activities have been omitted to prevent the book becoming unreasonably long. Answers have only been included if we wanted to illustrate or discuss a particular point they contained.

Space for answers

A related topic is that of providing space for the students to write an answer. In general we support the idea of leaving space, though there are some courses or activities where the amount of space needed would make the study booklet excessively long. Reasons for leaving space include the following:

- By writing an answer the student ends up with a well organised set of notes, which should be useful for revision.

- The amount of space can indicate the extent of the expected response.

- It is a strong suggestion that you want the student to take an active approach and write down an answer.

- White space is a good reader stopper: it makes the student stop and think rather than read straight on.

These last two reasons probably explain the finding that students are more likely to write an answer if space is left[1].

---

1   Lockwood, F. (1992) *Activities in self-instructional texts*. Institute of Educational Technology, UK Open University/Kogan Page.

Please note that we have either excluded or considerably reduced the space left after the original version of our extracts. We do not expect you to attempt the activities we have included.

Theoretical considerations

Though you will find occasional reference to research and theoretical support for the various uses of activities, such considerations are not the aim of this book. Our use of theory is generally implicit rather than explicit.

For a more theoretical treatment of the use of activities in open learning, Lockwood[1] is a good reference. In particular, he examines the assumptions made about activities by course tutors and relates these to the expectations and perceptions of learners. His own research results point to ways in which learners can be encouraged to use activities, and to the style of activitiy that learners are most likely to attempt.

One clear finding is that activities are less likely to be attempted if they are likely to take an unreasonable amount of time. This is perfectly understandable, given that students of open learning courses are often part-time students who also have jobs and/or families to cope with. It is, therefore, a good idea to make time expectations explicit (see Activities 2, 3, 11 and 27).

If students are expected to carry out activities, the demands made upon them should be realistic. For example, they should not be required to dash out every five minutes in search of new information. Where advance data gathering is necessary, or where materials or equipment not normally to hand are required, students should be given ample notice (see Activities 34 and 37).

---

1   Lockwood, F. (1992) *Activities in self-instructional texts*. Institute of Educational Technology, UK Open University/Kogan Page.

Activities should be relevant to the course and not inserted just because there has been no activity for a page or two.

However carefully the activities are designed, you should not assume that all students will do all activities. It is clear from the research of Lockwood and of Clyde *et al*[1] that there is great diversity in the ways that students use open learning materials. Some students will do all the activities while others will do few if any. Some will write full answers while others just think about the questions. Some work through in the order suggested while others jump around. This diversity in approach should not mean that activities are omitted or study strategies not suggested; rather that expectations are made explicit and features well signposted so that students can follow a study path which suits them.

Deep and surface learning

An area of research which has influenced us is the work on approaches to learning. Marton and Säljö[2] identified two discrete approaches to reading articles. Students adopting a *deep approach* concentrated on the underlying meaning of an article. The intention was to understand the real message of the reading.

Students who used a *surface approach* concentrated on surface features of the learning task, such as key words or phrases. Their intention was to memorise and reproduce elements which seemed appropriate. When asked about the content of the articles they tended to give detail from examples but had often not grasped the principle of the article.

---

1   Clyde, A., Crowther, M., Patching, W., Putt, I. and Store, R. (1983) How students use distance teaching materials: an institutional case study. *Distance Education*, 4, 1, 4-26.
2   Marton, F. & Säljö, R. (1976) On qualitative differences in learning: 1. Outcome and process. *British Journal of Educational Psychology*, 46, 4-11.

19

Since the initial characterisation of deep and surface approaches to learning it has been possible to apply these descriptors to academic tasks such as reading, writing and practical work in a wide variety of disciplines from school to university level and in many parts of the world. There has been some discussion of the meaning of deep and surface approaches in different contexts. Biggs[1] believes that there would be wide agreement among the numerous researchers, employing both qualitative and quantitative methods, that a student who adopts a deep approach:

- is interested in the academic task and derives enjoyment from carrying it out;

- searches for the meaning inherent in the task (if a prose passage, the intention of the author);

- personalises the task, making it meaningful to own experience and to the real world;

- integrates aspects or parts of task into a whole (for instance, relates evidence to a conclusion), sees relationships between this whole and previous knowledge;

- tries to theorise about the task, forms hypothesis.

A student who adopts a surface approach:

- sees the task as a demand to be met, a necessary imposition if some other goal is to be reached (a qualification for instance);

---

1 Biggs, J. (1987) *Student approaches to learning and studying.* Melbourne: Australian Council for Educational Research.

• sees the aspects or parts of the task as discrete and unrelated either to each other or to other tasks;

• is worried about the time the task is taking;

• avoids personal or other meanings the task may have;

• relies on memorisation, attempting to reproduce the surface aspects of the task (the words used, for example, or a diagram or mnemonic).

The learning approach a student adopts for a particular learning task is influenced by the student's motivation and the prevailing teaching context. Factors such as extrinsic motivation, lack of interest, reproductive assessment questions, formal teaching, a focus on transmitting information or excessively heavy workload have all been shown to make the adoption of a surface approach more likely.

An experiment which is relevant to this book was performed by Marton and Säljö[1]. Students were asked to read three chapters with questions interspersed after the first two chapters. The students were divided into two groups: one group was asked factual questions which demanded a surface response; the other group was asked questions which aimed to induce a deep response. The effect of the experimental manipulation was examined in interviews.

The authors report that the effect on students who were asked the surface level questions was quite uniform. These students paid close attention to detailed points in the chapters. For the group asked deep level questions, two approaches emerged. One set of students did use a deep approach as expected by the experimenters. The other set did not seek the meaning of the article but instead concentrated on remembering

---

1 Marton, F. & Säljö, R. (1976) On qualitative differences in learning, outcome and process II. *British Journal of Educational Psychology*, 46, 115-127.

short summaries of the text.

This experiment has a clear message for the design of activities. It is all too easy to induce students towards using a surface approach by consistently setting fairly trivial activities or those which require only recall of information. As most would consider this to be an undesirable outcome for their courses, setting activities requiring just information recall is clearly something to be avoided. Unfortunately setting questions requiring more meaningful responses does not guarantee that students will employ a deep approach. Consistently meeting questions which demand careful thought does at least send a message as to what is required in the course.

Chapter 1

Types of response

Short answer 1

Probably the simplest activity that can be used in open learning materials is the short answer, which we interpret to mean that the response can be anything from a word or number up to a paragraph in length. Most often it is used to check the students' grasp of a concept or process by giving them the opportunity to express their understanding in their own words.

We include this activity simply to stress that it is not always necessary to call upon a sophisticated technique in order to check understanding. It can be sufficient merely to focus their attention on key points by asking questions about them. You can provide correct answers or specimen answers where appropriate.

The gollowing example on page 26 is taken from a management subject which includes a topic on strategic planning. The activity is located just after the presentation of both text and a diagram outlining the strategic planning process. Consequently, the activity calls for more than just straight regurgitation of a definition. Students are required to interpret the diagram (see also Activity 28) and combine their interpretation with the textual material to explain the process. Naturally, a sample answer is provided for further reference at the end of the topic.

Using Figure 2.2 as a guide, this is an appropriate time to monitor your grasp of the process of strategic planning. Write a paragraph explaining the key elements of the process as illustrated.

extact: Management Perspectives, Deakin University, Geelong

Extended answer 2

If students are required not only to display an understanding of an idea, but also to apply their knowledge to particular circumstances, then a longer response may be required.

Note that it would be most unusual for the answer to a self-assessment activity to be more than a page or so. Anything longer than that, it can be argued, might be more suitably placed in an assignment. Of course, it is also possible to use such activities as assignments, though in that case sample answers would not be supplied!

The other obvious problem with extended answers is that, if they are not for submission in an assignment, their sheer length will discourage students from seriously attempting them. Thus we do not encourage their frequent application. They can be useful, though, when they also form the basis for discussions at tutorial sessions, should these be part of a course (see also Activities 40 to 46).

It is a good idea to give students some idea as to the length of the expected response. There are two ways to do this. The first is by leaving space after a question for the answer. The amount of space left can serve as an indication of the amount you expect the student to write as a response. The alternative method is to indicate how long you expect the student to spend on the activity. Activity 3 illustrates this latter approach.

The following example is from a post-graduate course in management for engineers. The particular subject is 'Design Management and Administration', and the activity is found in a section dealing with the use of sub-consultants.

It has been suggested, even predicted, that the design consultancy industry will develop to the point where there will be three or four 'big boys' having organisations larger than 1,000 people, and the remainder will consist of specialist small companies (boutiques) that will act as sub-consultants. Do you agree with this suggestion/prediction and, if so, what trends have you noticed to support this postulation? However, if you do not agree, on what trends do you base your opinion?

extract: Design Management and Administration, Association of Professional Engineers and Scientists, Australia.

Ticking boxes   3

If students are required to make fairly quick judgements about a situation, then a useful activity can be one that requires them to choose from among alternatives and to indicate their choice by placing a tick in a box or boxes. The advantage is that they can make their assessments swiftly and can indicate their preference without having to indulge in any unnecessary writing. This approach is also used in multiple choice questions (see Activity 4).

In the following example, students in a management training course for supervisors are asked to assess a number of short case studies, and to identify the forces at work from a brief list of alternatives. Notice that an indication of the time required to complete the activity is shown. Such suggested times can be useful, especially for novice learners, but care should be taken to avoid possible disadvantages. For example, students who continually find that they take longer to complete the activities than the suggested times may become discouraged.

• Time guide 8 minutes

Read these examples and tick the force you think helped to bring the changes about in each case.

• *Caroline Quigley had been a clerk at the old-established firm of Terence Gratton Ltd for twenty years. She knew her job so well she hardly had to think about it any more. Then one day the management decided the time had come to computerise all clerical functions. Caroline was put in the difficult position of learning to operate a computer and to do her job in a totally different way, or else face possible redundancy.*

Was this change brought about by:

Technology? ☐

Social factors? ☐

Economic factors? ☐

• *Polly Martin took over as Managing Director of a company making a range of products, including cosmetics. She wasn't particularly happy about the fact that the company used animals in some of its procedures for ensuring products were safe for the public to use. Polly undertook a large survey of the company's potential customers and the results suggested that the company's image would be enhanced if it ceased using animals in product testing.*

Was this change brought about by:

Technology? ☐

Social factors? ☐

Economic factors? ☐

• *John Frederick's bookshop was the only one in the growing town of Busbury and brought him a steady but unspectacular income. Then a new shop opened in the town, belonging to a large chain of bookshops. John wasn't particularly worried at first, as he felt he could continue to compete. Then John was dismayed to learn that the new shop was selling many of his most popular titles at a discount. Within a short time, John's shop was only doing half the business it had before. John was eventually forced to close his shop.*

Was this change brought about by:

Technology? □

Social factors? □

Economic factors? □

• *Kirsty Bright had run the wages section of a building company for years. Every week, Kirsty travelled with the Accounts Manager to the bank to collect a considerable sum of cash. One day, just as they had left the bank and were about to get in their car with the money, they were held up at gun-point by two robbers. Although they weren't hurt, Kirsty and her manager were really shocked and scared, and Kirsty said she would never again help to collect the wages. When the incident was reported to the senior managers in the company, they decided to stop paying wages in cash: all workers were to be paid by cheque.*

Was this change brought about by:

Technology? □

Social factors? □

Economic factors? □

extract: Managing Human Resources, NEBSM Super Series, Pergamon Open Learning, Oxford.

Multiple choice 4

The use of multiple choice questioning has a long and chequered history, and there is not space here to give detail of methods of construction of 'good' multiple choice questions[1]. Suffice to say that such questions should not be seen as an easy way out, as their setting can be extraordinarily difficult and time consuming. Nor should they be considered as suitable only for low level activities, as they can be applied to higher order application and analysis skills.

The example shown below is taken from an accountancy course, and the particular subject deals with accounting standards. The sample answer to the activity is also shown. Notice that not only does it indicate which is the correct response, it also explains why the other choices are incorrect. This illustrates how carefully the distracters have been assembled, designed in this case to reveal common errors made by novice accountants.

An item of equipment which is being leased has a useful life of 10 years. The guidelines of AAS 17 would indicate the lease should be classified as a financial lease if the lease is:

A cancellable, has a guaranteed residual value and is for a lease term of eight years.

B non-cancellable and provides for a guaranteed residual value that takes lease payments to 90 per cent of the fair value of the lease asset.

---

1 Useful guidelines for constructing objective tests, including multiple choice items, can be found in Gibbs, G., Habeshaw, S. and Habeshaw, T. (1988) *53 Interesting ways to assess your students*. Bristol: Technical and Educational Services.

C non-cancellable and, at the beginning of the lease term, the present value of the lease payments equals 95 per cent of fair value of the leased property.

D non-cancellable, has a guaranteed residual value and is for a lease term of six and a half years.

The sample answer at the end of the topic reads:

Correct answer: C (refer to paragraph 9 of AAS 17)

A is incorrect. Refer to paragraph 9 of AAS 17; the lease has to be non-cancellable in terms of paragraph 5(r) of the statement.

B is incorrect. The present value of the lease payments has to be taken into account.

D is incorrect; not for 75 per cent of useful life to the property.

There are many variations on the basic multiple choice format, and one other will be shown here. The example asks students to choose a number of correct responses from a list. It has been extracted from a Human Resource Management subject.

---

extract: CPA Core II, Australian Society of Certified Practising Accountants.

4. Which of the following questions should *not* be asked in an interview?

(a) What experience have you had with computers in your previous employment?

(b) Where did you obtain your qualifications?

(c) Mr Smith, why do you wear an earring?

(d) Are you married, Ms Jones?

(e) Can you tell us about your specific job responsibilities when you worked at IBM?

(f) What salary would you be seeking, should you be offered this position?

(g) I see you did some work for a church group. Does this mean that you are a Christian?

(h) Do you plan to have children, Mrs Allport?

(i) Why did you leave CMB after only six months?

The sample answer for this activity is:

4. The following questions are not appropriate, and can even be against EEO legislation and guidelines:

(c) Mr Smith, why do you wear an earring?

(d) Are you married, Ms Jones?

(g) I see you did some work for a church group. Does this mean that you are a Christian?

(h) Do you plan to have children, Mrs Allport?

extract: Human Resource Management, Deakin University, Geelong.

Calculations 5

Many disciplines involve calculations, so naturally students on courses in these areas are expected to do calculations—often numerous calculations. This is perfectly sensible: without practice students cannot hope to become skilled in performing calculations. Tackling a numerical example can also be a very good way to come to grips with a theoretical explanation.

In courses of a scientific or mathematical nature there is often a standard structure. A new concept is introduced with an explanation. Its relationship to other variables is explained, usually by deriving formulae. A sample calculation or two is then shown. The students are then expected to try some calculations themselves.

A straightforward example of this type of calculation is shown below.

A 240V supply passes through a bulb with a resistance of 1000Ω for 100s.

1. What is the energy consumed?

2. What is the power rating of the bulb?

---

extract: Science for Matriculation Studies, University of Papua New Guinea.

The above example is of the type which is very good for getting students started on tackling problems related to a new concept. They practice solving standard problems which they may subsequently have to do on a routine basis. Completing relatively straightforward problems can boost their confidence, which is especially important if they are studying at a distance.

There is a danger, though, when a course consists of nothing but questions of this type. Students can get into the habit of solving problems simply by picking what seems to them to be the most likely formula from among those encountered in the sample calculations. They then substitute the relevant numbers, after which it is purely a matter of algebraic manipulation.

This is fine if the aim is developing algebraic skills. However, most courses are more concerned with developing an understanding of the concept itself, and straightforward problems may not help in this respect. All too often it is possible for students to solve the problems by substitution and algebraic manipulation without having to think about the concepts at all.

When constructing a set of problems or calculations it is wise to keep this in mind. Perhaps start with a reasonably straightforward problem or two, but then try to include some which seriously challenge the students understanding of the underlying concept.

Two examples of more complex problems follow. The first poses a mathematical problem in an every-day context rather than in abstract mathematical nomenclature.

A newspaper boy has 82 houses on his round. He delivers *The Daily Post* to 20 houses, *The Times* to 66 and *The Guardian* to 56. Of those receiving *The Daily Post*, 6 take *The Times* and 8 take *The Guardian*, but only 2 subscribe to all three papers. What is the most popular combination of newspapers on the boy's round?

The second example also uses a realistic scenario. The problem does not assume that there is only one correct answer. It asks students to determine whether matrices can be evaluated and to interpret the result.

In a market survey for the greengrocery trade three ladies were asked how many lbs. of potatoes, carrots and apples they had purchased on their last visit to the greengrocers. Their responses are shown in matrix K.

Two greengrocers were asked to quote their current prices for these commodities in each of their shops and their replies are given in matrix L.

Purchase in lbs.
Potatoes/Carrots/Apples

Prices in pence/lb.
Shop C   Shop D

$$
\text{matrix K} = \begin{array}{c} \text{Mrs A} \\ \text{Mrs B} \\ \text{Miss X} \end{array} \begin{pmatrix} 2 & 1 & 2 \\ 5 & 2 & 3 \\ 3 & 1 & 1 \end{pmatrix}
$$

$$
\text{matrix L} = \begin{array}{c} \text{Potatoes} \\ \text{Carrots} \\ \text{Apples} \end{array} \begin{pmatrix} 10 & 8 \\ 8 & 7 \\ 12 & 16 \end{pmatrix}
$$

matrix K   matrix L

Determine whether KL or LK can be evaluated and, where possible, compute the product and give an 'interpretation' of the result.

Activity 18 discusses the issue of problems which might challenge students' conceptions of key phenomena. Activity 40 has a very good example of a mathematical problem which would definitely need students to think about the underlying concept. It shows also that mathematical calculations, and other calculations too, can be the starting point for discussion.

extracts: Armstrong, P.A. (ed.) (1977) *Polymaths book C: Sets, concepts and relations.* Cheltenham: Stanley Thornes.

Crosswords 6

A crossword can be a suitable device for checking the meanings of terms in a technical subject. As such, it provides some variety from simply writing definitions 'parrot fashion', or matching words with their meanings. The decision to use this type of puzzle should be taken with care, and be based on your knowledge of the students and the needs of the curriculum. It is unlikely that a crossword would be suitable for a postgraduate course, while it may be justified in certain certificate or diploma courses.

The following example of a crossword is taken from a higher certificate course in civil engineering for second language English speakers. The particular subject is Geotechnology, and, for a change, the key terms within a topic are checked by the use of a crossword.

Solve the following crossword puzzle. The questions are based on Readings 16.5 and 16.6. Try to complete it without going back over your reading material. The complete solution is printed in the answer section.

Across

2   This part of an earth dam is usually made of rock fill (3).

4   A man-placed soil (4).

7   Both the soil and piles are part of this (10).

9   Type of fill obtained by dredging (9).

11 Name for the source soil when using fill (6).

12 A clay which makes soil expansive (15)

14 This type of foundation carries the load of a structure to deeper soil layers (4).

15 The process of lowering the ground water level (10).

16 The part of the load of a building which includes furniture, people, machines, books etc. (4).

Down

1   Relatively dangerous kind of settlement (12).

3   This kind of dam is flexible and economical (5).

5   A deep foundation (7).

6   This content has to be just right when compacting (8).

8   This method achieves all the settlements before construction begins (10).

10 Not usually found in an earth dam, but you can get it when drilling in rock (8).

13 Name for a foundation slab (3).

extract: Geotechnology III, Hong Kong Polytechnic.

Matching lists 7

Another variation in testing students on their knowledge of basic terms and concepts is to use the process of matching lists. As the name implies, the activity involves providing a list of terms and a corresponding list of explanations or definitions which have been mixed up. The students are then required to match the lists.

The example given here is from a human resource management subject, the specific topic being Managing Rewards. Students are expected to be familiar with the terminology of reward management, and so were given the following activity.

Match the following terms with their definitions.

a   Bonuses   A   Incentive payments, whereby the seller or agent receives a flat amount of money or percentage of the sale price, on the sale of a product or service. A commission may be paid in addition to a flat retainer.

b   Commis-sions   B   *Ad hoc* or one-off payments made to employees who, after the fact, are deemed to have performed particularly well on something.

---

c	Flexible Package	C	Schemes whereby payments are made if the company achieves a particular level of profit. Some of the profit achieved above the threshold level is distributed to the eligible employees, as defined in advance.
d	Fixed Benefits	D	The name given to schemes which offer variable remuneration payments, or other specific rewards , for the achievement of specific objectives over and above what would have been achieved otherwise.
e	Incentives	E	Refers to the Total Remuneration plus grossed-up Fringe Benefits Tax required to be paid on the benefits.
f	Package, Total Package or Total Cost	F	The non-monetary provisions made available by an employer for the employee, such as the use of a company car, parking facilities and health insurance coverage.
g	Profit Sharing	G	The employees have some choice as to how their Total Package amount will allocated to various ends, such as school fees, travel and entertainment.

---

extract: Human Resource Management, Deakin University, Geelong.

Fill in blanks 8

Most people probably think of fill-in-the-blank activities as paragraphs of text with words missed out from time to time. The fancy name for these is cloze tests. An example is:

> Most people probably think of fill-in-the-blank activities as paragraphs of text with .... missed out from time to time. The fancy name for these is ....

We would not encourage you to use activities like this. They can give students the idea that all you want them to do is to remember key words. The students are therefore encouraged to adopt a surface or reproductive approach to study tasks.

More beneficial uses of a fill-in-the-blank format are for leading students through a calculation, or through a standard way of setting out experimental results which you want the students to use. It is helpful to lead students through calculations when they first meet a new type. To prevent students from using the same formula for all subsequent calculations, introduce a few novel twists.

The example includes both a common calculation and a standard layout of experimental results from a chemistry titration. The course included several titrations so it was important that students learnt how to calculate results and used an appropriate format for presenting their data.

Data table

Mass of steel wool ....grams

Total volume of solution made up in the flask ....cm^3

Burette readings

final volume   .... cm^3

initial volume   .... cm^3

vol. solution used   .... cm^3

In the space provided, calculate the following:

1. The number of moles of $KMnO_4$ which reacted with the Fe^{2+}.

2. The number of moles of Fe^{2+} which reacted, the moles of Fe, and the mass (in grams) of the iron which reacted.

3. The percentage of iron in your original sample of steel wool.

---

extract: Introductory Chemistry B, University of the South Pacific.

Student summaries 9

A useful device for consolidating student learning of a topic is to allow them to construct a summary of the material. They are thus encouraged to structure the material in a way which suits them, rather than the author of the course. A sample answer can be provided, or a listing of the points that should be covered, but the aim should be to get them to consolidate learning in their own way.

Student summaries are also useful in integrating readings or texts into study materials. Students can be asked to study a reading, and then provide a summary of the main points. In the following example, the original summary was removed from a journal article, but was later revealed as a sample answer, as indicated below.

Summarise, in a couple of paragraphs, the major points made by Beutell in Reading 3.1.

The feedback to this activity, at the end of the topic, reads:

The summary provided here is the original from Beutell's article. Naturally yours will differ, but the thrust of the message should be the same.

'The computer age has created excitement in the field of PHRM. Besides handling "routine" work quickly and accurately, computerised human resource information systems can empower the personnel function by developing inputs for the strategic planning process. Additionally, the computer is creating new jobs, helping to monitor personnel operations, individualising training programs, and providing access to a vast array of information. The advantages of computerising PERM include productivity gains, inexpensive computer technology, speed and accuracy, user-friendliness, and organisational impact. These advantages appear to outweigh the possible human costs of automating (e.g., technostress). Nevertheless, the effects of computerising need to be assessed periodically.

As the use of computers in most areas of PHRM, including college and university personnel courses, increases, the demand for human resource data administrators and computer literate personnel managers will rise sharply. Computer knowledge can be a comparative advantage for career development of PHRM professionals.'

The next example shows another way of using student summaries, but takes it a little further by applying the summarised material to a situation with which students are familiar. The study material just before the activity had presented explanations of the major research findings on the characteristics of managerial work. It had drawn attention to seven distinct characteristics.

---

extract: Human Resource Management, Deakin University, Geelong.

Summarise and apply each of these seven characteristics to your own job as a manager (or your manager's job). To what extent does each apply to the job?

Characteristic of Managerial Work	Applicability to Position		
1.	Low	Medium	High
2.	Low	Medium	High
3.	Low	Medium	High
4.	Low	Medium	High
5.	Low	Medium	High
6.	Low	Medium	High
7.	Low	Medium	High

extract: Management Perspectives, Deakin University, Geelong.

Making glossaries 10

Many disciplines have their own jargon and technical terms. Like it or not, students need to know these technical words if they are to make headway with understanding the subject matter. Many text books therefore include a glossary. However, the course can be made more active if the students compile the glossary. The set text or readings almost always have explanations of key terms so it is not too difficult to ask students to write their own definitions of selected terms.

The example comes from a course in law, a discipline which has its fair share of terminology. The example uses the case study format described in Activity 24. The students are asked to think about passages from the set text in terms of a case study used throughout the subject. In the example the first task after reading the prescribed passage is to note down the meaning of important terms.

Reading

Chapter 10, Pages 182 to 184

Section 10.2—The Doctrine of Apparent Authority

Activity

With reference to Case 1, mother has read the facts and decision of Freeman and Lockyer v Buckhurst Park Properties (Mangal)

Ltd. but does not understand some of the terms used. Advise mother as to the meaning of the following terms:

quorum of the board

actual authority

representation

extract: Hong Kong Company Law, Hong Kong Polytechnic.

Tea break   11

Inexperienced students often have poor study habits. A common mistake is to get carried away with initial enthusiasm and study for hours on end. Attention spans of even the best students rarely last much longer than one hour. Beyond that attention tends to drift and little if anything is understood.

With this in mind, you can help novice students by suggesting that they break up periods of study into manageable sessions with short breaks in between.

Some courses divide the material into short sections and explicitly suggest that students take a break after each section.

This is a very easy chapter, don't you agree? If you are happy with this section, don't stop, turn to section 2 now.

. . .

Well, you have finished another section in this package now. This section is a bit long, but the principles of the treatment programme for this condition are rather basic. Now relax, have a cup of tea, and then check your answers on page 14.

It is worth noting that some activities of the type which we are exemplifying can in themselves serve as a break, especially where they

---

extract: Deformities of the Hip Joint, Hong Kong Polytechnic.

involve more than just sitting and reading. Indeed, such activities can be inserted into open learning materials specifically to enforce a break at appropraiate points.

Chapter 2

Didactic conversation

Simulated dialogue 12

Many open learning courses are conducted at a distance. The students spend the majority of study time working by themselves through a package of study materials. This means that they miss a lot of the social and academic interaction of a face-to-face course. Direct interaction can be built into courses through the inclusion of tutorials, teletutorials, individual telephone counselling, electronic mail and other communication channels.

It is also possible to simulate a conversation with students through a study package. Holmberg[1] coined the term *didactic conversation* to describe this type of dialogue. The aim is for the tutor to develop a rapport with the student through the study package. A simulated conversation of this type can introduce an element of human contact into isolated study. It is also a way of guiding the student towards an active approach towards the subject.

The simulated dialogue often takes on a question and answer format. The tutor poses a question in the text and then provides feedback on the answer the tutor presumes the student will give. The discussion can then flow on to the next point.

The extracts used as examples in this book are almost all from the printed component of study packages. There is a pragmatic reason for this: it is much easier to reproduce materials printed in a book than those recorded on audio or video tapes. However, do not interpret the preponderance of print-based examples as meaning that the particular activities illustrated are only suitable for printed materials. Many could be used with other media. Simulated conversations can be particularly

---

1   Holmberg, B. (1985) *Status and trends of distance education.* Lund: Lector.

successful on audio tape. The tutor's voice has a more human quality than the written word, however informal the writing style.

This brings us to an important point in the writing of simulated dialogue or any other instructional material for that matter. Do not use a dry, formal, impersonal writing style! You are not writing an academic paper or a formal textbook.

Adopt an informal writing style more akin to the conversation you might use in a classroom. Allow your personal thoughts to creep into your writing. Try to put yourself in the position of an isolated student studying in the evening after a day at work. Would you want to read a dry, formal document in those circumstances?

As this is a fundamental principle underlying the writing of self-instructional packages, two examples will be given.

The 'generation gap'

Since the 1960s, the term 'generation gap' has been widely used in the U.S. to characterise the relationship of contemporary adolescents and their parents. As compared with the 'silent generation' of the 1950s, contemporary adolescents are described as rebellious and capable of being openly critical of their parents and the establishment. They are also believed to have conflicts with their parents most of the time, viewing their parents as stubborn and old-fashioned, disapproving of the ways they treat them and receiving little support from them.

What were the most serious conflicts between you and your parents during your adolescence? How deep was the generation gap then?

You may have pointed out that there was a gap between you and your parents during your adolescence, but it never reached the proportion frequently proclaimed by the mass media.

Contrary to popular belief, much research conducted from the 1960s to 1980s in the U.S. also suggests that the generation gap is grossly exaggerated. The following extract examines the validity of the generation gap in some detail.

Notice how the writer has asked a question and anticipated an answer from the student. As the student has been asked to relate the answer to personal experience there is not one correct answer. Even if there were, dialogues do not develop well if the text consists of a series of questions followed by definitive answers. Students tend to read on to the answer without bothering to consider their own answer to the question.

In a typical organisation individuals generally find that the group norms require them to make minor adjustments which do not cause any real concern. Occasionally, particularly in the early stages, they may find that they face a real conflict when the group wishes them to act in a way which is in fundamental opposition to their personal wishes. The conflict is particularly severe if the group is a reference group.

Imagine that you are at a tutorial and your tutor asks you whether you approve of, say, the Australian Broadcasting Commission's television programmes. Assume that you do not approve of the A.B.C. but you are the last to be asked and everyone else in the tutorial group approved enthusiastically. What would you say?

If you felt very strongly you may 'stick to your guns' but if you were even slightly doubtful you would probably go along with the group. And so it is in organisational situations. In many organisations—perhaps most—the Marxist doctrine of 'them and us' (the owners and the employees) is still very much alive and group pressures on the young to join 'us' against 'them' are very real. I have been in this situation and I can assure you that the pressure is real.

The writers of the two extracts have tried to personalise the questions to ensure that the students do not simply 'go along with' their text. The first asks the students to consider their own childhood. The second describes a scenario and asks the students how they would react.

Both extracts anticipate the most likely answer of the students. In both cases, though, the feedback or comment is sufficiently open to allow for alternative responses. Notice the use of personal forms of language. The writer refers to himself as 'I' and talks of his personal experiences. The student is referred to as 'you'. It is easy to interpret the written passages as personal conversations.

first extract: Social Environment and Human Behaviour, Hong Kong Polytechnic.
second extract: Organisational Behaviour 1, University of Tasmania, Launceston.

Relating to personal experience 13

A good way to make students think about new ideas you raise is, each time you introduce a new concept, to ask them to think of an example that they know about or have experienced. You can simulate a discussion with them by asking the students to relate to their own example each time you raise a new aspect of the concept in general terms.

A course on organisational behaviour used this strategy. Each time the author used a new way of describing an organisation the students were asked to think how the description applied to an organisation they knew.

The informal organisation

Informal organisation is hidden

Whereas the formal organisation is visible, the informal organisation tends to be hidden, or at least difficult to identify. If you were to visit an organisation which was strange to you, the Personnel Officer or Public Relations officer would probably give you a conducted tour of the building. The Personnel Officer would do so because it was part of the formal duties and would show you the outwardly visible formal organisation. If the Personnel Officer left you for a while to have afternoon tea with some of the staff, you might well get your first glimpse of the informal organisation. Quite likely you would be told 'what it's really like', and it could be suggested to you that people in the organisation in positions of formal authority 'did not have a clue what goes on'. You might notice that ten minutes was the prescribed time for a tea break, but realise that it had lasted twenty minutes. If you asked you would be told something like 'no one worries too much' or 'we (the informal organisation) decide when afternoon tea is finished'. If you decided that some of this behaviour was a display for your benefit you would be correct. Nevertheless, it would be an example of the informal organisation in action.

Can you identify this type of behaviour in any organisation with which you are familiar?

Is there a sense in which you believe that you 'know what goes on behind the scenes'?

In this example the relationship between the writer and student is developed by the informal writing style as well as the questioning technique. The scenario described and the comments of the workers make it easy to relate the concept of the formal and informal organisation to personal experience.

extract: Organisational Behaviour 1, University of Tasmania, Launceston.

Relating to work experience 14

Many open learning courses have been developed, and continue to be developed, with the aim of improving workplace skills. Naturally, such courses must prominently feature activities that relate the course content to workplace experience. If students are expected to come to a deep understanding of the concepts with which they are faced, it is vital that they be given plenty of opportunity to stop and reflect on what they are learning, specifically as it applies to their day to day work.

It can be difficult, however, to incorporate activities that relate course material to work experience if the course is a general one in terms of its student intake. In such circumstances, it often cannot be assumed that the students are in employment or have ever been employed (in which case, activities such as those described in Activity 13 might be more suitable). So, the decision to use this type of activity has to be taken with care.

For the following extract, though, the decision was easy, perhaps even mandatory. The course was specifically designed for those employed in the finance sector, and students were thus frequently called upon to reflect on links between the course materials and their experience of work. The extract is taken from a basic management subject, under the topic of 'Organising'.

Consider the following ground rules for delegating:

• carefully choose who you delegate to

• make the assignment clear

- agree on standards of performance

- encourage and allow independent action

- show trust in the other person

- give feedback on performance

- help out when things go wrong

- don't forget your accountability

Describe a delegating situation in which you have played a part. Explain how its success or failure depended on one or more of these 'ground rules'.

extract: Management Perspectives, Deakin University, Geelong.

Reflection and action 15

The idea of reflection followed by action can take the previous notion of relating to work experience a step further. That is, not only should students relate what they are learning to their own situation, but they can also be encouraged to reflect on the implications and take action in their life at work. This general concept has been championed in recent years by Schön[1], whose notion of reflection-in-action has been applied to professional education.

Of course, not all students will go through the entire process, right through to implementing some change or attempting to have some change made at work. However, our experience tells us that some will, and this makes the inclusion of activities of this type both worthwhile and potentially rewarding.

The example shown here is taken from a management course for those employed in the service sector, and is part of a topic on 'Operations Management, Monitoring and Control'.

(a) Using, as a guide, the six steps outlined above for a manufacturing audit, design an audit process which could be applied to the operations department of your own organisation. (Disregard the components of the manufacturing audit which do not apply to a service provider.)

Step 1

Step 2

---

1   Schön, D.A. (1987) *Educating the reflective practitioner*. San Francisco: Jossey-Bass.

Step 3

Step 4

Step 5

Step 6

(b) Discuss your audit process with an operations manager in your organisation. If possible, attempt to have your process implemented.

---

extract: Management Perspectives, Deakin University, Geelong.

Maintaining a journal 16

The requirement for students to maintain a journal while studying has become a part of many courses, and is used for a variety of purposes. Chiefly, the aim is to encourage students to reflect on their learning, and chart their progress as they grow and change.

Such journals have also found their place in open learning courses. For some, they are purely for the students' own reflective purposes, while others build them in to the assessment process. In this extract, the journal is definitely part of assessment, comprising seventy per cent of the final mark. It is taken from a course in family medicine for general practitioners, and the particular subject is Palliative Care. The introduction to the use of a journal is as follows.

Each session will include a number of activities. The main one will be reading but audiotapes and a videotape will also be used. Keeping a journal will contribute significantly to your assessment at the end of the unit. In it we would like you to record clinical details of cases, your reactions to and feelings about care of dying people and some of the tasks set in the various sessions.

Other more specific details concerning the maintenance of the journal are also provided. Two activities which involve the use of the journal are as follows.

Please read 'Helping your patients deal with questionable cancer treatments' (Reading 4).

In your journal, describe your understanding of 'alternative treatments' and how you counsel patients in this area.

There is an exercise designed to help us deal with the issues of death and dying in which we are called upon to imagine our own death. The following headings may help you to do this:

• At what age will it occur?

• Where will you be, and at what time of day?

• Who is with you?

• What are they saying and what would you like them to say?

After this exercise, record your feelings in your journal. Did you find the exercise useful? Do you think it is helpful in understanding how you care for those who are dying?

extract: Palliative Care, Monash University, Churchill.

Exposing misconceptions 17

In the field of science education there has been a lot of research into the conceptions students hold of basic scientific phenomena.[1] Some of the results are quite disturbing. Gunstone and White[2] used experimental demonstrations as stimuli for revealing students' conceptions of basic physics phenomena. In one, students were asked to predict whether a heavy or light ball, dropped together, would reach the ground first. The majority of students predicted that the heavy ball would reach the ground first, revealing an Aristotelian conception of physics.

The surprising aspect of this study was that the students were successful university physics students. They must have been taught Newtonian concepts of gravity and passed examinations including questions on its applications. Yet the simple demonstration revealed that many of the students still clung to an Aristotelian conception of the world.

Findings like this have a certain shock value, but there are strong implications for all teaching. Osborne and Wittrock's review[3] of the science education literature noted three major findings from this work. First, even before science instruction, children form firmly held views of scientific concepts, many of which are quite different to current scientific theories. Secondly, these misconceptions are surprisingly persistent, being observed in much older students after considerable science teaching. Finally, pupils often construct an individual

---

1   For reviews of this research see West, L.H.T. & Pines, A.L. (Eds) (1985) *Cognitive structure and conceptual change.* New York: Academic Press. and Ramsden, P. (Ed.) (1988) *Improving learning: new perspectives.* London: Kogan Page.
2   Gunstone and White (1981) Understanding of gravity. *Science Education,* 65, 291-299.
3   Osborne, R.J. and Wittrock, M.C. (1983) Learning science: a generative process. *Science Education,* 67, 4, 489-508.

conception of a scientific phenomenon which is very different from that intended by the teacher.

The last two of these findings suggest that it is important to concentrate on teaching fundamental concepts. This conclusion should certainly not be restricted to science education. There has been less research into non-scientific disciplines, but that which has been conducted suggests similar findings.

The research into student misconceptions shows that merely presenting a concept is insufficient if genuine understanding is desired. The physics students in the example above were taught the relevant concepts, possibly several times. Yet the students' conceptions can be diametrically opposed to the concepts they were taught. Clearly it is difficult to establish new conceptions, alter existing conceptions or replace naive conceptions with more sophisticated ones.

A three-phase process seems to be required to bring about conceptual change.

1. A process for diagnosing existing conceptual frameworks and revealing them to the student.

2. A period of disequilibrium and conceptual conflict which makes students dissatisfied with existing conceptions.

3. A reconstruction or reforming phase in which a new conceptual framework is formed.

The first step towards conceptual change is, therefore, the identification of existing conceptions. Questions of the type used in research into student conceptions and misconceptions of fundamental concepts would be suitable for this step. The questions should pose a genuine test of the students' understanding of the concept. Usually the questions have asked students to interpret everyday phenomena in the light of their knowledge of the discipline.

To illustrate the teaching of fundamental concepts two contrasting activities will be discussed.

An elephant weighing 40 000 N has feet of area 1000 cm^2 (= 0.1 m^2). What is the pressure on the ground?

$$\text{pressure} = \frac{\text{force}}{\text{area}}$$

$$= \frac{40\ 000\ \text{N}}{4 \times 0.1\ \text{m}^2}$$

$$= 100\ 000\ \text{Nm}^{-2}$$

$$= 1 \times 10^5\ \text{Pa}$$

Questions like this are very common. Students normally answer them by adopting a simple procedure. They decide which of the formulae they have remembered is appropriate. They work out which numbers correspond to the variables in the formula and substitute into the equation. From then on it is simply an algebraic exercise.

There is nothing fundamentally wrong with problems of this type. They do indeed provide practice in manipulating data and solving numerical problems. The one above requires an understanding of powers of ten and the use of units. However, it should not be assumed that successfully solving a numerical exercise implies an understanding of the concepts represented by the equation. A student could solve the above problem without having any real understanding of pressure, force or mass.

Now consider an alternative activity which might stimulate thought about the underlying concepts. A single activity may not be enough to change a strongly held conception, but if a course concentrates on fundamental concepts, and if activities of this latter type predominate, then conceptual change is possible.

If a lady wearing stiletto heeled shoes and an elephant walk across a piece of soft ground, which is likely to leave the deepest footprints?

Your immediate reaction may well have been the elephant. The elephant would have a greater mass than the lady. The total force or weight that it exerts on the ground would be greater than the lady's. But is it really appropriate to consider just the weight?

You may have started to think about how the forces are applied. Elephants have big feet. Their large weight would therefore be distributed over a relatively large area. The lady's weight, though, would all be applied through the very small area of the stiletto heel.

Which is the appropriate physical concept to apply?

Try using the following data to determine which does the most damage. An elephant weighing 40 000 N has feet of area l000 cm^2 (= 0.l m^2). A lady weighing 400 N has stiletto heels of area 1 cm^2 (1×10^{-4} m^2).

To determine the depth to which the foot and heel will sink you need to consider the area over which the force is applied. The elephant is very heavy but the force is applied through its large feet. The effect on the ground is spread over a large area. The weight of the lady, however, is concentrated onto the point of the stiletto heels. Her weight is less but it acts through a much smaller area.

Pressure is the physical quantity which relates force and area of contact. If you have not already done so work out the pressure applied by the elephant and the lady.

elephant **lady**

pressure $= \dfrac{\text{force}}{\text{area}}$ pressure $= \dfrac{\text{force}}{\text{area}}$

$= \dfrac{40\ 000\ \text{N}}{4 \times 0.1\ \text{m}^2}$ $= \dfrac{400\ \text{N}}{2 \times 1 \times 10^{-4}\ \text{m}^2}$

$= 100\ 000\ \text{Nm}^{-2}$ $= 200 \times 10^4\ \text{Nm}^{-2}$

$= 1 \times 10^5\ \text{Pa}$ $= 2 \times 10^6\ \text{Pa}$

The elephant exerts larger *force* because it is much heavier, but the lady's heel exerts a much bigger *pressure* because of its smaller area! The lady's heel would sink further into the ground.

Chapter 3

Learning from texts

Introduction

When writing an open learning course you can either write the entire package yourself or make some use of existing materials. Often much of the content for a course which is to be developed will already be available in existing textbooks or could be compiled as a collection of readings. It is obviously easier to make use of existing materials than to write everything from scratch yourself. Students can have the advantage of learning from well-produced texts and reading the original work of the best writers in the field.

If you do decide to use existing materials then the open learning package becomes a study guide to a textbook or collection of readings. A companion volume published by TES deals with writing study guides.[1]

As the term suggests, the function of a study guide is to guide students through the text or readings you have selected. Usually this means providing activities so that students actively engage the material in the selected readings. Activities 18 to 23 show a variety of activity types for inclusion in study guides to direct students' reading of specified content and to encourage an active approach to reading the text.

---

1   Kember, D. (1991) *Writing study guides*. Bristol: Technical and Educational Services.

Questions   18

The most common form of activity used in study guides is probably the question. You write a series of questions to direct students' attention to key concepts, to make them think about issues or practise procedures which have been taught. Comments on the text and additional information can be interspersed between the questions at appropriate points.

The given example continues the didactic conversation style discussed in Activity 12. In this case, though, textbooks or readings are used as the main source of material. The study guide writer and student can now engage in a conversation about set readings.

In the extract short manageable sections of the text are specified. The first question directs students' attention to the main point of the reading. The comment which follows leaves students room to formulate their own views on the topic.

Oakley takes a position almost 'opposite' to that discussed so far and suggests that roles are determined by cultural norms. Her position is that most often seen as typical of the 'feminist movement'. The evidence she offers is persuasive although the limitations are obviously those which apply to any cross-cultural comparison. By that I mean that the argument which suggests a programmed (biological) development may still be valid if the 'norms' have continued over great periods of time. Nevertheless the points made by Oakley must be seriously considered particularly when allied to the views of Bettelheim.

Read Haralambos pages 375-377.

#6-8 What is Friedl's hypothesis for male dominance?

The position taken by Friedl is particularly interesting and leads us in the direction of the current situation of male and female roles in contemporary organisations. I find the position that she has adopted attractive as it covers the middle ground between the extremes of cultural and biological determination.

Read Haralambos pages 377-379.

I am not impressed with Ortner's argument where she develops the nature versus culture idea, but am prepared to acknowledge the virtue of her position to which Haralambos alludes on page 379.

#6-9 Do you agree?

extract: Organisational Behaviour 1, University of Tasmania, Launceston.

Tutor looking over shoulder 19

A good analogy for a study guide is that of a tutor looking over the shoulder of a student studying the set textbook or collection of readings. When writing a study guide try to think of yourself as a tutor in that situation.

* Which parts of the text would you point out for particular attention?

* Which might be skipped over or not read at all?

* Are there any sections which need clarification or additional comment?

* Can you think of any local examples which would make the material more interesting and relevant?

* Can you anticipate any problems the student might raise or clarification questions you would be asked?

* What activities would you suggest to the student to practise the concepts taught?

* What feedback would the activities need?

The extract below covers a number of these points. Firstly the difficulty of the readings is discussed. This can be important for those studying in isolation at a distance. They probably have no fellow students to discuss the reading with, so if they have found it difficult they could conclude that they are not good students. Students attending a class could discuss the reading amongst themselves and so would realise that everyone had the same problem. They might be able to work together to interpret the reading.

After discussing the difficulty of the reading, key concepts are highlighted.

The first two questions ask students to relate the concepts in the reading to their own school (the course is for school teachers). The other two questions ask the students to analyse and compare models.

Young's book, however, does not make easy reading for beginners, especially those without a sociological background. For this reason as well as others, it would be more fitting for you to start with Philip Robinson's synopsis of this perspective in Chapter 7 of his book Perspectives on the Sociology of Education (London: R.K.P., 1981).

Reading–Robinson, *Perspectives on the Sociology of Education.*

Even this chapter is still rather condensed, and you are advised to pay special attention to the following concepts:

- strong and weak classification;
- collection code versus integrated code;
- visible versus invisible pedagogy;
- rationalist models of the curriculum;
- reflexive models of the curriculum;
- curriculum-as-fact;
- curriculum-as-practice;
- relational models of the curriculum;
- the hidden curriculum.

Is your school's curriculum marked by a strong or weak

classification?

Is your school's (or your own) pedagogy visible or invisible?

Robinson presents three types of curriculum model. Which one do you prefer and why?

Do you think that these models are incompatible with each other?

extract: Social Environment and Human Behaviour, Hong Kong Polytechnic.

Headings 20

When the content is supplied in the form of a set text or a collection of readings it can be useful to suggest that students make their own notes from the set readings. They then actively extract what is important from the text and end up with a succinct account for future reference and revision.

Activities 20–23 suggest ways to guide students towards the key concepts in the readings. Such activities should help in the development of reading skills. The stress is on the recognition of the underlying message of the author.

A simple way to show the structure of a section of text is to provide students with a set of headings. If space is left after each heading the students can write their own notes under each heading. The end result is hopefully a well structured set of notes. As with the questions in Activity 18, comments and additional material can be interspersed between headings at appropriate points.

The example which follows consists of a short comment followed by the specification for the reading. A main heading and three sub-headings are then shown for note taking. The amount of space left under each heading can be used to indicate the approximate amount to be written.

Common stock

Preferred and common stock financing are well explained in your text and not much can be added. Only the topic of common stock and pre-emptive rights is complex enough to deserve further elaboration.

Reading 14-7

Basic Financial Management, pages 551 to 558

- Common Stock

Make notes on the main features of common stock under the headings below.

Rights of Common Stock Owners

    (a) Income

    (b) On bankruptcy

    (c) Voting

extract: Financial Management, University of Tasmania, Launceston.

Tables 21

Tables are commonly used to order information in a convenient and succinct manner. Information in conventional linear text can often be summarised in a table. Students can be asked to construct such tables as an activity. To do so they must read carefully the original text and think about its structure.

The skeleton of the table is usually given and students asked to complete the boxes. Tables are particularly suitable for tasks such as:

• sorting into categories

• identifying the elements of alternative models

• arranging examples in a convenient form

• comparing and contrasting competing theories.

The first example asks students to make a summary (see Activity 9) of information about fabrics in the form of a table.

Summarise the main features of the fabrics you have just learned about by filling in the following table. To assist you, the first example has been done for you.

fabric	raw materials	weave	end-uses
corduroy	*cotton/ polyester*	*special with plain or twill back*	*trousers, jackets*
denim			
drill			
etc.			

Courses based upon a collection of readings can ask students to compare and contrast the alternative views, models or theories of a number of writers. What is more, the students can be asked to examine the original work of the authors rather than a commentator's view of their work. It can, though, be difficult for students to compare and contrast alternative views. A way to help students to analyse the articles is to provide a table as a framework for noting contrasting positions on key issues or concepts.

extract: Knowledge of Materials, Hong Kong Polytechnic.

The example below is from a curriculum theory course. The table is designed to help students compare the views of prominent writers on moral or values curriculum. The original table was an A3 foldout so that there was a reasonable amount of space for the students to make notes.

Writer	What is the rationale for moral education?	What methods are advocated?	What would the curriculum look like?
Scriven			
Crittenden			
Jarolimek			
etc.			

extract: Curriculum Theory, University of Tasmania, Launceston.

Graphic outlines 22

When reading an instructional text, better readers and those who employ a deep approach to learning normally start by surveying the text to get an idea of the main points. They normally look at main and sub-headings and other features. Less efficient readers continue to employ the technique they were originally taught—reading from start to finish—regardless of the type of text or the purpose for which they are reading.

Students can be helped to learn and use the survey technique by asking them to complete graphic outlines. A graphic outline shows the structure of a section of text, such as a chapter, as delineated by the main and sub-headings. Boxes are left with appropriate amounts of space for students to note down the main ideas covered by each of the designated sections.

Graphic outlines can be used to help students develop their reading skills. Initial graphic outlines might show headings and perhaps a summary of main ideas. Progressively the information given should be reduced so as to encourage the students to survey the text for themselves. Even for skilled readers a graphic outline can be a useful activity in the from of an aid to analysing and summarising complex texts.

Morris and Stewart-Dore[1] advocate the use of graphic outlines within a structured programme to develop skills for reading in content areas. Their book contains several examples of graphic outlines and other

---

1 Morris, A. and Stewart-Dore, N. (1984) *Learning to learn from texts: Effective reading in the content areas.* NSW: Addison-Wesley.

strategies for developing reading skills. A wider overview of graphic organisers in texts is provided by Hawk, Macleod and Jonassen[1] .

The example of a graphic outline on the next page was taken from a course in personnel development. Students were asked to read a specified section of the course textbook and to summarise material on evaluation objectives in the graphic outline. The various boxes in the diagram reflect the structure of the information given in the textbook.

---

1   Hawk, P., McLeod, N.P. and Jonassen, D.H. (ed.). *The technology of text (volume 2): Principles for structuring, designing and displaying text*. Englewood Cliffs, New Jersey: Educational Technology Publications.
extract: Personnel Training and Development, University of Tasmania, Launceston.

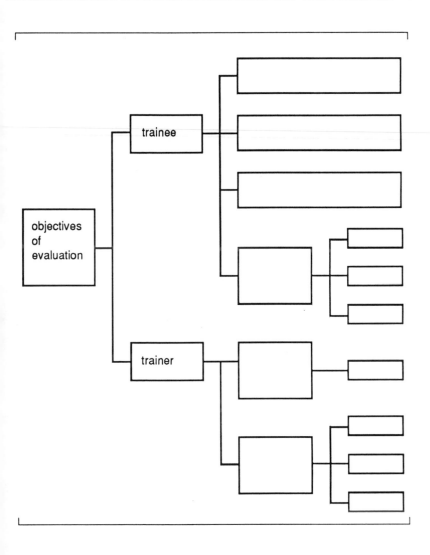

Reading instructions 23

Many courses give students lengthy reading lists. Often the suggested readings are of quite different types or serve varying purposes.

- Some explain fundamental concepts and need very careful study. It can be necessary to read sections several times.

- Other parts might be read at the pace you would read a novel.

- Still others might give examples or illustrations which could be skimmed through fairly quickly.

- Some authors like to include extensions to a basic course which need to be read only by certain types of student.

- Sometimes lists of readings are given just to demonstrate that the author is familiar with the most recent or the most advanced work in the field. These probably do not need to be read by anybody.

Unless someone tells the students, though, they may not be sure which of these categories a particular reading falls into.

The chosen extract, included on the following two pages, gives very full guidance for studying a chapter.

A suggested approach to study

In order to gain the maximum benefit from your study for this chapter, I recommend you adopt the following approach or programme of study:

1. Quickly read the whole chapter (but not the answers!).

2. Note the most important topics and organise your time accordingly.

3. To gain an *impression* of the historical context for the topics you will be studying in this chapter, I strongly recommend you do the following:

Skim read either Bailyn et al., *The Great Republic,* Chapters 1-2,or Carroll and Noble, *The Free and the Unfree,* Chapters 1-2.

Note the *key features* of the period discussed in those chapters.

But remember—the key words here are *an impression* and *skim read.* Don't take too long over this task; keep any notes you may take very brief.

4. For each topic:

    •   Read my introduction and then note the references you will need and your study tasks.

    •   Carefully read my comments on the topic and the in-text self-assessment questions.

- Read the set references and attempt to answer the self-assessment questions.

- Compare your answers with mine in the answer booklet. If they differ markedly, try to explain why.

- If you find yourself stuck on a self-assessment question, read my answer and then try to work out how I arrived at it. But only do this if you're stuck despite a genuine attempt to answer it yourself first.

5. When you've mastered the topic move on to the next one.

extract: History 5A, University of Tasmania, Launceston.

Case studies 24

Case studies are a good way of transforming the general, abstract or theoretical material in textbooks to local applications. Text book writers usually have to cater for as wide an audience as possible to maximise sales. It is, therefore, unlikely that any examples and applications they give will be closely related to the experience and needs of your students. Local case studies provide an opportunity to take the general principles from the text and apply it to a scenario appropriate for your course.

Information on one or more cases can be given in the study guide. As each major topic is covered in the text it can be related to the cases by devising an activity. You ask the students to apply the principle or concept they have learnt from the textbook to the realistic situation of the case study. If necessary the case information can be built up as new topics are introduced. This can make the course interesting as the students follow the development of the characters and story-line.

In the following example, the case study approach was used throughout a course on company law. Students were asked to apply the principles from a textbook to two cases which eventually interacted. The first case concerned a small printing company which was setting up business.

This case information was given at the start of the first unit. For each subsequent unit the case is updated to provide material relevant to the topic covered in the unit. The case becomes a developing saga. The other case used in the book concerned a larger company so that topics not appropriate to a small family business have a realistic context.

Case 1

In 1990 father, mother, son and daughter decided to rent a small workshop, purchase four old printing presses and to run their own printing business. Father and son had previously worked for a large printing company which became computerised and so made a number of its staff redundant. They are both very familiar with traditional printing presses and are of the opinion that such printing is still in demand and could provide them all with a good income and standard of living. Mother has worked as a book-keeper throughout her working life. However she has recently experienced great difficulty in obtaining employment because she also has no experience of computers. Daughter has recently graduated with a degree in design.

Furthermore, father has signed a two-year lease for the workshop; the rent is $5,000 per month and at the end of the two years the lease may be renewed subject to a review of the rent.

Son has paid a deposit of $10,000 for the printing presses: he is presently arranging for their transportation and has agreed to pay the balance of the purchase price, $50, 000, on the last day of the month or the day the machines are moved, whichever is the sooner.

In this unit it is assumed that father, mother, son and daughter have decided to form a company limited by shares and that they are all busy working to that aim.

Most activities in the study guide refer to one of the case studies.

With respect to case 1, advise the family as to the documents which they must submit to the Registrar in order for their printing business to be incorporated.

In relation to case 1 and assuming that the family have formed a company, Family Co. Ltd., by what legal processes may that company obtain the lease of the workshop?

If father has obtained insurance against fire and theft for the workshop and the lease is transferred to the company, will the insurance policy remain effective?

The course objectives also refer to the cases. They were formulated as questions relating to the cases and positioned at the end of each chapter. They function as an active checklist on what has been learnt in the chapter.

What did you learn in this unit?

With reference to case 1 you should be able to discuss with the family and to advise them on the following questions:

To what extent will father, mother, son and daughter be regarded as promoters given that they have decided to form a registered company?

What documents are required for registration of a company?

What is the legal significance of a certificate of incorporation?

Are promoters liable on contracts which they enter into on the company's behalf but before company is actually incorporated?

To what extent may father, mother, son and daughter avoid being personally liable for contracts which they sign on the company's behalf before they receive the certificate of incorporation?

extracts: Hong Kong Company Law, Hong Kong Polytechnic.

Chapter 4

Learning from teaching resources

Drawing graphs 25

Illustrative material should not only be an integral part of most open learning courses, but should also be fruitfully and creatively used in the activities. As with text, illustrations and diagrams can form the basis for both the checking of basic understanding and for the development of interpretative and other skills.

Drawing graphs is a basic skill required in many courses across a wide range of subject areas. The following example is taken from a certificate level civil engineering course: the specific topic is soil mechanics. This activity is given well into the subject, by which time students are expected to be familiar with graphical methods.

Below is a table showing the test results of a cone penetrometer method. Plot the data on the graph paper provided and determine the liquid limit of the soil.

Test details:

Proportion of sample on 425 mm BS test sieve 10%.

Soil conditions: natural moisture content, air-dried, unknown.

Soil equilibrated with water for 24 hours.

Test number	1	2	3	4
Type of test	LL	LL	LL	LL
Initial dial gauge reading (mm)	0	0	0	0
Final dial gauge reading (mm)	12.8	15.3	16.8	26.2
Cone penetration (mm)	12.8	15.3	16.8	26.2
Container number	45	112	103	84
Mass of wet soil + container (g)	44.14	52.47	54.21	53.05
Mass of dry soil + container (g)	41.03	49.84	51.33	50.57
Mass of container (g)	30.46	41.45	42.23	43.29
Mass of moisture (g)	3.11	2.63	2.88	2.54
Mass of dry soil (g)	10.57	8.39	9.10	7.22
Moisture content (%)	29.4	31.3	31.6	35.2

Results: liquid limit (LL) =

extract: Geotechnology III, Hong Kong Polytechnic.

Labelling diagrams   26

Where the introduction of new terms and concepts involves diagrams, it is often preferable to build the activities around such diagrams, rather than to ask for prose descriptions. Such labelling can be applied to diagrams that students have already seen, or they may be required to identify certain features in novel situations or previously unseen figures.

The following activity is taken from the same soil mechanics subject mentioned in the previous activity. Students had been supplied with a series of photographs and diagrams dealing with the major types of soil transportation, but had not seen the diagram in the activity before.

The diagram below shows the distribution of transported soil types in Hong Kong. Complete the diagram by filling in the labels.

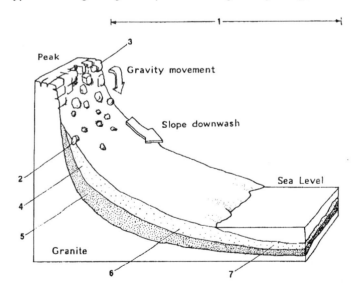

1. T_____ soil

2. B_____

3. F_____ granite

4. Mid-levels colluvium

    g_____,

    s_____,

    s_____,

    c_____.

5. Weathered granite zone _____ soil

6. River alluvium

    sand,

    silt,

    clay.

7. m_____ c_____

extract: Geotechnology III, Hong Kong Polytechnic.

Interpreting graphs 27

The interpretation of graphs naturally takes learning a step further. In most courses involving graph work, the interpretation of graphs is more important than the ability to plot them. This higher level skill can be introduced by example, with instances of interpretation being provided before the students try some examples themselves.

The extract overleaf is taken from an economics subject, wherein students are introduced to the analysis of supply and demand. As a guide, students are shown diagrammatically the effects of an increase in demand, before being given the following problem of interpreting an increase in supply.

Assume that the market for X is initially in equilibrium, as shown in Figure 1.13 at point *a*. Then assume that at each price level suppliers decide to increase supply in an effort to boost revenue. Complete Figure 1.13, showing the new supply curve, prices and quantities and any excess supply/demand.

Provide a commentary of no more than 100 words.

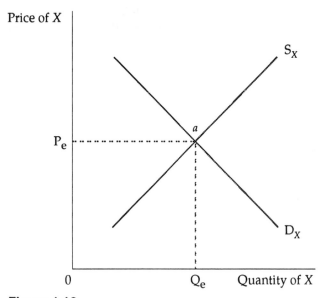

Figure 1.13

The following sample solution is given at the end of the topic.

Answer Suppliers deciding to increase supply can be depicted by an outward shift in the supply curve from Sx to Sx´ (shown below). Note that this assumes suppliers are willing to increase supply by an equal amount at each price level. Initially, there would be an excess supply, with supply increasing to Q´ and demand remaining at Qe. This would eventually be removed as price falls, with demand and supply converging at equilibrium point *c*, with price Pé and quantity Qé.

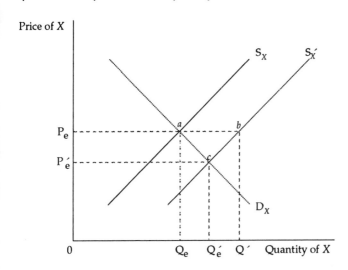

Interpreting diagrams   28

For many subjects, the interpretation of diagrams is as important as the interpretation of text. It is a step beyond simply labelling features and can take many forms, a popular one being the interpretation of cycles that are part of the study of geography, for example. An instance was also provided in Chapter 1 (Activity 1—Short answer), which was an interpretation of a combination of diagram and text.

In the example shown on the next page, students in a geotechnology subject are focusing on soil mechanics. They are required, after a short study of weathering, to interpret the major features of a diagrammatic representation of a slope.

Examine the diagram below which shows weathering in different environments and conditions. Answer the following questions in the space provided.

1. Why are there more cracks or joints at P than at Q?

2. Where do the boulders at R come from?

3. Why are there so few boulders at S?

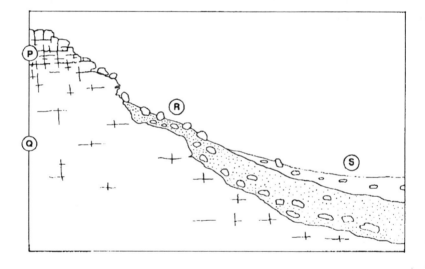

extract: Geotechnology III, Hong Kong Polytechnic.

Psychological tests   29

It is well known (especially by publishers of popular magazines) that most of us enjoy responding to questionnaires that reveal something about our personalities. This may equally be true of students enrolled in open learning courses. Thus a ready resource for the construction of activities is the existence of a multitude of standard tests and questionnaires, many originating in the psychological literature.

One that is well known and widely used in educational circles is the Kolb Learning Style Inventory[1]. The inventory measures the student's relative emphasis on four learning modes: Concrete Experience, Reflective Observation, Abstract Conceptualisation and Active Experimentation. These are then combined to give an indication of which of four learning styles the student most closely approximates to: Accommodator, Diverger, Converger or Assimilator.

It is a fairly simple, straightforward test that can be self-analysed to reveal one's orientation to experiential learning. As such, it can be used at a variety of levels and in a variety of ways depending on the level and aims of the course. It also has the advantage of being available in computer form, so that students can simply respond to a series of items and then be presented with an analysis of their learning styles.

Kolb's inventory requires students to rank words from nine sets of four words. The first few item are as follows:

---

1   Kolb, D. (1985) *Learning-style Inventory*. Boston, Mass: McBer.

Rank the words in each set by putting a 4 by the word which best characterises your learning style, a 3 by the next best, a 2 by the next best and a 1 for the least accurate descriptor of your learning style.

1. [ ] discriminating [ ] tentative   [ ] involved   [ ] practical

2. [ ] receptive   [ ] relevant   [ ] analytical [ ] impartial

3. [ ] feeling   [ ] watching   [ ] thinking   [ ] doing

4. [ ] ...

Audio tapes 30

Audio tapes have long been used in open learning materials, but have always been somewhat under-utilised. In past years, this was probably because they were too often simply used as an 'add-on', or for some enrichment of otherwise tedious prose. More recently, audio tapes have become a victim of the 'old' technology syndrome, viewed as rather out of date compared to the newer and more exciting technologies.

However, audio tapes can be used very fruitfully and successfully as core components of open learning courses, particularly as it can usually be safely assumed that the students will own or at least have access to a tape player. Additionally, they also give students the chance to do some study when in situations where reading isn't possible: audio tapes can be listened to when driving a car or when exercising, for example.

Good applications of audio tapes to open learning materials include recordings of interviews and debates, explanations of complex diagrams, the outlining of the logic involved in mathematical expressions and proofs, and the describing of procedures and processes for students involved in 'hands on' applications.

The first example presented here is from a subject dealing with accounting standards. Note that the course prepares accounting graduates for professional examinations, so the materials are by no means 'low level'. Audio taped discussions are used extensively in the course materials, including the activities.

In this case, the taped information is aimed at equipping the students to tackle the final part of an accounting problem. There is a discussion (of just under four minutes duration) between the two authors of the subject, who help students to locate relevant material and show how the material can be applied to the problem.

a   Write out, with brief explanatory notes, the year three tax-effect journal entry that To and Fro Ltd would need to process.

b   What special information about future income tax benefits should To and Fro Ltd disclose in each of the three years? Assume the balance at 1 July 19X0 was $10 000 dr.

c   Assume that no accounting entry to future income tax benefit was made at 30 June 19X1 with respect to tax losses because it was expected at the time that there was no possibility of recoupment of these losses; however, it was expected that sufficient future income could be available to absorb the present balance of future income tax benefit.

i   How should the subsequent recoupment of the tax losses be treated and disclosed? Present the required journal entries and disclosures for 19X2 and 19X3 (refer to paragraph 23(a) of AAS 3).

Listen to the tutorial-on-tape.

ii   What does the required treatment of the recoupments imply about the tax journal entry that should be processed in the loss year? Supply the required journal entry and disclosures.

Our second example is from a sociology course, which provides a series

extract: CPA Core II, Australian Society of Chartered Practising Accountants.

of audiotapes to form the basis of group discussions of key questions (see also Chapter 6). As well as part of the explanation of the use of the tapes, one of the sets of discussion questions is also included.

Using the audiotapes

For each tape you will be receiving a list of discussion questions to guide your listening. I suggest that you use the tapes as follows:

1. Read over the discussion questions before you hear the tape. That way you'll have an idea on what to focus.

2. As you listen to the tape take notes on the content. The information on the tapes is presented at a fairly rapid rate so the best you can probably do is take notes. In other words, it is unlikely that you will be able to answer the discussion questions as the tape is being presented.

3. After the tape is heard, you should collaborate with the members of your group to develop answers to the discussion questions.

I recommend this format because it allows you to pool your individual understanding to develop more confident, complete responses to the issues presented in the audio tapes.

Audiotape discussion questions: 'The working class conservative: image and reality'

1. What is the difference between 'conservatism' and 'traditionalism'?

2. What are the three major sources of political beliefs and how do they exert their influence?

3. Why does upward mobility have little effect on political conservatism?

4. What evidence suggests that there is a weak link between a traditionalist outlook and a conservative political affiliation?

5. Why is it that stereotypes of the working class poorly fit the facts?

extract: Sociology, University of Manitoba, Winnipeg.

Using computer programs 31

An obvious activity associated with computer programs is the writing of them. Such an activity is clearly appropriate for computer programming courses but it is difficult to see their relevance to other courses. Before examining activities using computer application programs, which do have a much wider relevance, let us briefly consider an example of an activity which asks the students to write a computer program.

The example is taken from a course which teaches students to write Pascal programs.

Write a program to find the average mark of a set of examination marks. The marks are in a text file called *results*, are real values, and there can be more than one mark given per line.

The file *results* could look like:

```
98.3 47.8 21.2
82.3
49.7 62.3 48.6 61.7
50.8
82.7
```

---

extract: Intermediate Pascal, University of Central Queensland.

Using application packages

Writing computer programs is an important activity for programming courses but not applicable to many others. Activities using application packages on computers can have relevance to a very wide variety of disciplines. Many professionals use a computer as a routine tool, so it would seem appropriate for courses in these disciplines to make use of programs which are commonly used. Here are some common examples of the routine use of computer application programs.

• Word processing packages are used for drafting and revising text.

• In the field of business, spreadsheets and databases are routine tools.

• Engineers and designers use Computer Aided Design programs.

• Numerical data is often manipulated and turned into graphs and charts with spreadsheets.

• Statistical calculations are invariably performed with statistics packages.

• Information is sought and reports are compiled from data stored in large databases.

When a discipline or profession uses computer applications such as these, activities involving the applications can hardly be left out of courses if they are to be relevant and up to date.

Use of computers can pose logistical problems for open learning courses as students need access to computer hardware and software. On-campus students usually have access to computer laboratories. Where students are dispersed off campus the problems are greater. For students at a distance various solutions to the access problem have been tried.

- Study centres have been provided with either microcomputers or terminals to central computers.

- Students have been loaned a microcomputer.

- It is a condition of entry to the course that students own or have access to a particular type of computer.

- Students on a course can be assumed to have access to a particular brand of computer because the course enrolment is confined to a particular type of student. For example, some education courses are restricted to teachers in an area where all schools have computers of a limited number of types.

- It is assumed that students will be ingenious enough to gain access to a computer, possibly with some help from course tutors.

- Some combination of the above.

To some extent the access problem will resolve itself since the more the computer becomes a normal everyday tool, the more students will have access to them. Open learning students are often mature professionals in positions using computers and application programs. However, because students have access to a computer does not mean that their computer will run any software you might provide. There is a wide variety of computers in use and most only run software designed for particular families of computer. Even with computers of the same type, some may be unable to run a piece of software because they are of different configurations. MS-DOS type machines, in particular, vary greatly in memory size, disk storage capacity and graphics boards.

If you solve your hardware access problem you may still have software access problems. If your course includes student exercises using standard application programs, the students must have access to that software. You can treat it as a textbook, but some software is quite expensive.

The example given requires students to make use of an application program for linear programming. The course introduces students to the capabilities of linear programming and the program itself through a series of problems based on the nursery rhyme about Jack Sprat.

Purpose of linear programming

Most practical problems are concerned with optimisation. That is, we have to find the best way to do something; the way which produces the most profit, or which takes the least time or money. Quite often these problems involve a choice between several activities, where each activity uses scarce resources. Problems of this type are called *linear programming* problems, where *linear* refers to the type of equations used to express the problem.

Take a simple case, that of the nursery rhyme:

> Jack Sprat could eat no fat,
> His wife could eat no lean.
> So between the pair of them
> They licked the platter clean.

Suppose that Jack has to eat 3 kg of lean meat each week, and that his wife has to eat 1 kg of fat. Furthermore, their butcher only sells the following three types of meat:

Lamb Chops at $5.00 per kg, comprising 30% fat and 70% lean (ignoring any bones);

Mince Steak at $4.00 per kg, comprising 20% fat and 80% lean;

Scrag end of Mutton at $1.50 per kg, comprising 80% fat and 20% lean (again ignoring any bones).

What meat should they buy each week in order to minimise their bill?

The students were shown how to solve this, and other more complex problems, using the linear programming program.

---

extract: Computer Applications, University of Tasmania, Launceston.

Video tapes   32

As with audiotapes, videotapes can be used creatively and usefully within open learning materials. The best examples are those which integrate the video with the text, rather than have it as an add-on, or use it simply as'enrichment'. The choice must be made whether to create new video material, use existing material, or make some combination of the two.

The following example is taken from a B.Ed. degree. The particular subject involves extensive use of video, in a variety of ways, some of which are explained. One of the many tasks which involve the use of the video is also included.

Videotape

Parallel to the course outline, Part 1 and Part 3 of the study guide are on a videotape. This provides source material, such as extracts from classrooms, and comments about the course by the course team. You need the videotape to complete some of the tasks in Part 1. A video index is provided at the end of Part 1.

The videotape is not a program or film, but provides a range of resources that relate to the course in different ways at different points. One of its functions is to serve as a way of talking to you about the course. It contains a series of numbered clips, short sections of tape that you will need in order to work on particular tasks. When you need to refer to these clips, a video icon will appear in the margin.

Task (45 mins plus viewing time)

Watch Clip 11, which is a set of extracts from different classrooms. You will find it useful to review Clip 9 before watching the first extract, which records a xylophone lesson taken by (name omitted). See video index at the end of Part 1 for a list of the extracts.

Make notes on some of the things that happened in each class. The next task will require you to recall these extracts and make various judgements about them in terms of a range of criteria.

---

extract: Classroom Processes, Deakin University, Geelong.

Home experiments   33

Practical work is considered essential for most science and technology courses and important for other disciplines too. Open learning courses which left out the normal practical component would be considered of little value. Many open learning courses insist that students attend residential school sessions to do the necessary practical work. Activities 52 and 53 deal with practical work in such sessions.

At a residential school session students would have access to sophisticated laboratory equipment. Experiments would be supervised by a tutor who could teach students appropriate techniques and ensure that the experiments were carried out safely. Clearly some experiments could only be performed in a proper laboratory with the necessary equipment.

It is also possible for students to do a wide range of experimental work at home. One advantage to the students is that the expense and inconvenience of attending residential schools is avoided. There are educational benefits too as experiments can be located at appropriate points within the course so that practical work reinforces theory, or a discovery learning approach can be used. There is no need to wait until the residential school before doing all the practical work in one block.[1]

Science courses which expect students to do experiments at home commonly supply students with a home experiment kit containing necessary equipment and chemicals. It is also possible to do a lot of experiments with material readily available in the home. If household items are used then it helps students perceive the relevance of science and technology.

---

1   For a discussion of home experiments or residential schools see Kember, D. (1982) External science courses: the practicals problem. *Distance Education*, 3, 2, 207-225.

The example chosen is one which relies entirely on household items. It also illustrates a discovery approach to science. By making observations students are led to deduce a physical relationship: that pressure increases with depth.

For this activity you need an empty plastic container, e.g. one for cordial or cooking oil.

Make 3 equal holes in the vertical part of the side using a nail

- one near the top
- one in the middle
- one near the bottom.

Now fill the container with water.

What do you see?

What does this tell you about pressure and depth?

extract: Science for Matriculation Studies, University of Papua New Guinea.

Field work 34

Field work has always been considered an important component of subjects like biology, geography and geology. It is also often necessary for students on courses like engineering, social work and hospitality management to visit the type of establishment they are being trained to work in. Sometimes these experience visits and field trips are less vital for adult students on open learning courses as they are already working in the area. Field trips, though, are still essential parts of some courses and there is no reason not to have them just because the students are at a distance.

A reasonably lengthy extract is given to show that discovery learning in a field setting is possible if well constructed instructions are given. For this biology field visit the instructions are precise enough to ensure that students will be able to complete the field experiment unaided, yet open enough to cater for a variety of field settings and to permit the students to engage in hypothesis testing.

Organisms of your grassland area

Investigate the following hypothesis:

'No two organisms have exactly the same way of life'.

Materials

Clipboard
Hand lens
Sweep net

---

3 jars
10 mls 70% ethanol

Procedure

Answer the following questions about 4 different animals you can find in your grassland community. Observe closely several specimens of each animal and enter your observations on the record sheet.

1. How does the animal obtain the food which it eats?

2. How does the animal protect itself, i.e. locomotion, defence, offence? (behavioural adaptations)

3. What special body feature does this animal have that gives it an advantage in living where it does? (structural adaptations)

To assist you in discovering answers to the three questions, conduct the following tests on each animal.

a. Watch it where it is for 3 minutes without disturbing it.

b. Observe its habitat closely (the habitat is the place where the organism lives).

c. Note the special situation of the animal in relation to sun, wind and rain.

d. Touch the animal with a stick and observe its reaction.

e. Examine the animal noting any distinctive structural adaptations.

You may need to capture the animals in order to study them. For small animals use the insect sweep net and stun them as instructed in Exercise 3. N.B. Avoid any dangerous animals such as snakes.

Enter your findings on the following record sheet (small sketches may be of assistance in recording some information).

	Animal 1	Animal 2
Name of Animal		
Sketch of Animal		
How the animal obtains its food (if you don't actually see it eating you can get a clue by examining its mouth parts with your hand lens)		
How the animal protects itself		

extract: Introductory Biology B, University of the South Pacific.

Part B

Activities in group meetings

General considerations

Most open learning courses have some meetings. They can be face-to-face meetings or meetings at a distance by teleconference. Teleconference meetings are almost always quite short but the face-to-face meetings can vary considerably in length from a tutorial, lasting an hour or two, to residential schools of a week or more. Some open learning courses are also conducted *in situ* so the amount of contact is even longer. For convenience we have referred to all of these meetings as tutorials and assumed reasonably short meeting times. If a course has more meeting time available it can be thought of as a series of shorter tutorials.

It is our contention that successful tutorials result from advance planning, preferably at the time the course is planned and the study materials developed. If the tutorials are planned at this time the tutorials and the study package can form an integrated learning experience.

Asserting to the importance of planning educational events is far from novel. Trainee teachers are told to draw up plans for each lesson, usually in some detail. Lecturers write lecture notes, sometimes detailed down to every word. All curriculum and instructional design models involve some type of planning, even if they disagree over sequence or the primacy of planning elements.

Somehow tutorials or telephone tutorials for open learning courses often seem to escape such planning. The study package can be finished before any thought is given to whether there will be tutorials. Tutorials may be held because it is the norm at the institution, without any real thought being given to what will happen in them, or the point in the semester at which they would be most effective. Students are told just that 'There will be a tutorial at place X, at time Y for course Z'. Is it any surprise if few attend?

Alternative approaches are again shown through a series of examples. Tutorials are characterised according to the main type of teaching which takes place. It is recognised that the categorisation is far from discrete. Many if not most tutorials will contain parts of one tutorial type and elements characterised by another type. Other tutorials will be best characterised as hybrids.

Each section starts with a general discussion of how the type of tutorial can be integrated into an open learning course. An actual example of that type of tutorial in an open learning course is presented. Relevant extracts from study booklets are shown to illustrate the way in which the tutorial activities were introduced through the study package.

In this part of the book the term tutorial is taken as including both face-to-face and telephone tutorials. The discussion, at the start of each section, considers any special considerations which apply to telephone tutorials because of the nature of that medium. The examples are from a mixture of face-to-face and telephone tutorials. In most instances the principles illustrated could be applied to either type of tutorial.

The activities given in this part of the book are certainly not restricted to open learning courses. They can be used in tutorials and seminars in conventional courses. The benefits of planning are definitely not confined to open learning courses.

Chapter 5

Student and tutor interactions

Arranged study groups 35

As already mentioned, successful tutorial groups don't just happen; they are planned. This is just as true for student led groups as it is for tutor led groups. It is most unrealistic to expect that students, given each other's names and contact numbers, will simply get on with it themselves. So, if course planners want students to meet in groups, careful planning is required. Better still, if the group activities are an integral part of the course, they will happen.

In the example presented here, students were all teachers enrolled in an upgrading course. It was believed to be essential that the students worked together to look at their own and each other's teaching, and so the activities in the course reflected this concern. The students were divided into 'groups of five', and the following series of tasks in the course materials exemplifies how they were expected to work together.

'Fives'

Students will be grouped in 'Fives'. As far as possible these will be groups of five students! But odd numbers and course deferments may mean smaller groups and some regrouping of students part way through the course. Members of each Five must communicate regularly and read and comment on each other's work. This group work is a course requirement and for this reason your name and address cannot be withheld from the Five.

Tutorial support

The Fives form the basis of a tutorial support system. You are required to telephone the other four students in your group every month. As well as being placed in a Five, you will be given a

---

number from 1 to 5. Each month a tutor will be contacting one member of your group. The first month it will be the person who has been given the number one, the second month number two, and so on. In these telephone conversations you will be expected to report not only your own responses to the course and any problems that have arisen, but also any news, questions or comments from the other four members of your group.

extract: Classroom Processes, Deakin University, Geelong.

Computer conferencing 36

Electronic mail is a means of sending messages from one computer to another via telephone lines. The computers are usually connected to the telephone network by devices known as modems. A message typed on one computer can then be transmitted to one or more other computers.

The message can be received by the other computer even if the recipient is not in or is using the computer at the time—an advantage over the telephone. The recipient reads the message the next time the electronic mail box is opened. Conversations, therefore, take place over a period of time—the technical term is asynchronous.

Computer conference systems are based upon electronic mail. One-to-one messages can still be sent, but it is also possible to send one-to-many communications and to have a group discussion.

A one-to-many message might be sent by a tutor to all students enrolled in a course. It could, for example, be an administrative message such as a mistake which had been discovered in a study guide or a change to a schedule for submitting assignments.

For isolated distance learners the computer conference facility has the greatest potential benefit as it permits students to join in a discussion with fellow students and tutors. A topic for discussion can be defined and a tutor might seed discussion by asking for comments on a reading, posing questions or making a thought provoking comment. Participators can then add their own comments or messages on the topic. Often the input will be a direct response to another comment, so a discussion builds up.

A difference between a face-to-face discussion and one by computer conference is that the latter is asynchronous, so comments do not have to follow a logical sequence in time as they do in a face-to-face meeting. The usual practice is to number messages. When students log-on they can then send a response to a particular numbered message even if others have posted messages in the mean time. The conference is not, therefore, restricted to a strict linear format as is a verbal discussion.

Computer conferencing does, therefore, offer the isolated distance learner a chance to interact with fellow students and participate in an academic discussion. Each student can participate at times which suit them. Participants have time to think of good comments—the stunning repartee that you always think of after the discussion is over.

A computer conference, though, certainly does not provide the same quality of social interaction as a face-to-face meeting. Mason[1] believes that such conferencing should not be seen as a substitute for face-to-face meetings or even telephone contact. If it was it would always be seen as a poor substitute.

Most of the other ideas and activities in this book can be adopted easily. Introducing computer conferencing is a major implementation exercise. Attention has to be paid to each of the following four aspects:

- hardware
- software
- logistics
- training the user.

The lower down the list the more attention is needed, contrary to most computer implementations.

The logistics of hardware and software access for open learning courses has already been discussed in Activity 31. Almost any computer can be

1   Mason, R. (1988) Computer conferencing: a contribution to self-directed learning. *British Journal of Educational Technology*, 19, 1, 28-41.

used for electronic mail provided the user has or acquires a modem. While reasonably high proportions of students have access to some sort of computer, far fewer have a modem.

Setting up and training students to use a computer conferencing system is a major topic which should be seriously examined before any commitment is made. The paper by Mason cited earlier is a useful entry to the literature. Other helpful papers are by Castro[1] and Phillips[2].

1   Castro, A. (1990) AARNet and Australian tertiary distance education. *Distance Education*, 11, 2, 213-230.
2   Phillips, C. (1990) Making friends in the 'electronic student lounge'. *Distance Education*, 11, 2, 320-333.

Involving family or workmates 37

Evaluation of many open learning courses has revealed that students often share what they are learning with those who are close to them, especially family and workmates. It is not surprising, then, that some courses choose to build this in as an explicit part of the learning process. It can have multiple benefits, including a 'sounding board' effect, an opportunity for shared reflection or gaining the opinion of others, and the chance to undertake activities that require more than one person.

This extract is taken from a course for teachers. The subject, *Classroom Processes*, contains a series of tasks which require the teachers to reflect on physical and other aspects of classrooms. Of interest is the way in which photographs are used to relate the material to what is happening in each classroom. As the tasks unfold, the teachers are encouraged to interact with a variety of others, including those in their study group (see Activity 35), as well as family or friends.

It should also be noted that the tasks are later used as part of the assessment for the subject (thus helping to ensure that the tasks are completed!). A selection of the tasks (omitting Task 16) is as follows:

Task 14 (Advance planning needed)

Obtain a set of photographs of you teaching in your own classroom. Ideally, you should enlist a colleague or student to take these for you. The object is to depict your working environment, to illustrate your way of working and to provide a context for looking at your teaching.

Task 15 (Advance planning needed)

Send one copy of each set of photographs to two people in your Five (we will call them A and B). You might want to enclose a brief letter, but at this stage try not to say too much. Let the photographs speak for themselves. With each set of photographs you send to A and B include the name and address of someone else in the group (C or D) to whom each of your correspondents can send the photographs before returning them to you.

Task 17 (15 minutes)

Using your own observations and the comments you have been sent, write three general statements about classrooms.

Task 18 (15 minutes)

Having previously shown the photographs (and perhaps their responses) to some of the people who apppear in them, or to your friends, relatives or others, write a report on their responses.

Task 19 (10 minutes)

Note any evidence of different perspectives in the interpretation of the photographs.

extract: Classroom Processes, Deakin University, Geelong.

Open agenda tutorials   38

In an open agenda tutorial a lecturer or tutor answers questions raised by students relating to areas of the subject they have found difficult or not understood. This is obviously a valuable type of tutorial in that it focuses on difficulties defined by students. The sessions are interactions between small groups of students and a lecturer/tutor, so have suitable characteristics for telephone tutorials.

Tutorials of this type can turn into disasters with new groups of students. The tutor might ask if any students have any problems, only to be faced with a deadly silence. The students may well have many problems but feel inhibited from asking questions because of shyness when faced with a new group. Mature students new to tertiary study can find it difficult to articulate their problems because they seem so overwhelming.

In a telephone tutorial problems of shyness will be compounded if the students are unfamiliar with the medium. Periods of silence, which are merely embarrassing in a face-to-face tutorial, become quite distressing in a telephone tutorial when the students are somewhere on the end of a telephone line—or are they really there at all?

When dealing with new groups of students therefore, we recommend starting with one of the other, more tightly structured, types of tutorials. Student problems usually emerge from the woodwork as the session progresses. As the group develops confidence the tutor can ask students whether they wish to raise any problems. If desired the element of structuring can be diminished to allow more room for student initiation of the agenda, once the group feel comfortable with each other.

Pure open agenda tutorials are more likely to be successful with students in the second or subsequent years of a course, especially if they have met at a residential school. Even these tutorials need planning. The first necessary aspect of planning is timing the tutorials in relation to the expected schedule for students to work through the study package. Factors to be taken into account include:

- resources available
- difficult areas in the study materials
- the timing of assignments
- even spacing to maintain student pacing
- whether an early tutorial is needed to cope with initial problems
- preparation for examinations
- public and institutional holidays.

Part of a typical plan, in the form of a study schedule, is shown in the example..

Once the tutorials are assigned to slots in the study schedule, each tutorial can be seen as relating to a part of the study materials. The students can then be told which parts of the course will be covered by each tutorial.

Advance planning is also necessary for telephone tutorials, especially if the subject area has any visual content. Difficulties with telephone discussion of visual matter can be reduced by:

- specifying a section of the subject for attention in the tutorials

- asking the students to have study guides and text books at hand

- ensuring that questions and answers relate to formulae or diagrams in those booklets.

The example for this section concerns a quantitative geography subject.

The first extract, on the next page, is part of the study schedule given in the subject outline. The study schedule shows that the telephone tutorials were scheduled in advance taking into consideration the relative difficulties of the content in the chapters. The tutorials were evenly spaced to introduce an element of pacing. At the first tutorial students can raise any concerns about the first assignment. Feedback on the first assignment can be given at the second tutorial, where students can also discuss problems with the second assignment.

Exact dates and times of tutorials were given in the subject outline, if they were available at the printing date. If the information was not available at the time of printing, it was sent to students in a separate tutorial information notice. Students were also given information about the tutorial at an appropriate point in the study booklet (see the second extract). The telephone tutorials were arranged with participants on home phones so the administrator needed to know which students were participating. Hence the need to send in a registration sheet.

STUDY SCHEDULE

Chapter	Week Beginning	Chapter Title	Assignment	Telephone Tutorials
1	25 Feb	Location		
2	4 March	Spatial Distribution		
3	11 March	Location Models (1)		Telephone tutorial 1
4	18 March	Location Models (2)		
5	25 March	Spatial Relationships	Assignment 1 due	
6	1 April	Spatial Diffusion		
7	8 April	Spatial Interaction		Telephone tutorial 2
8	25 April	The Regional Concept	Assignment 2 due	
	22 April	MID SEMESTER BREAK		

Telephone tutorial

- The first telephone tutorial for this subject is planned for the next week.

- Exact dates and times can be found in the subject outline.

- If you wish to participate please send off the registration sheet for Telephone tutorial 1 as soon as possible, if you have not already done so.

Tutorial topics

This tutorial will cover any topics from Chapters 1 to 3 of the study guide which you found difficult or would like to explore further. The topics are:

1. Location
2. Spatial distribution
3. Location models (1)

Planning for the tutorial

- Look through Chapters 1 to 3 and note down any questions you wish to raise in the telephone tutorial.

- Make sure you have at hand your study guide and textbook.

extract based loosely on: Geography 1, University of Tasmania, Launceston.

Surgeries   39

The notion of surgeries is reasonably self explanatory: students are given the opportunity to visit a tutor during 'surgery hours' to consult on a particular problem with their studies. It is not usually necessary to make an appointment, just to turn up at a nominated session. Such surgeries are usually made available at times that are suitable to the majority of students, and in places that allow easy access.

Naturally, surgeries are not common for courses for which the student population is widely dispersed. The following extract, however, is taken from Hong Kong, where no student is too distant from a study centre. The two notes are part of the explanatory notes for a first level mathematics subject.

In addition to tutorials and telephone contact with your Tutor you can obtain help with problems on M101 at Mathematics Surgeries. During these sessions, one or two tutors will be available to see students to discuss their problems and difficulties. This service will be provided on a first-come-first-served basis, although the number of tutors involved will be increased if demand justifies it.

Surgeries will be held on Wednesday evenings (except public holidays) and during weekends when there is no tutorial or day school. Dates of weekend surgeries are given in the Presentation Schedule. There will be two tutors covering the period from 6 to 9 pm on Wednesday and only one tutor from 2 to 4 pm on weekend surgeries.

You are strongly encouraged to make use of this facility if you

---

need to or if your tutor recommends it. It is hoped that these surgeries will provide students with plenty of opportunity to get help with the course in between tutorial/day schools.

extract: M101 Student Study Guide, Open Learning Institute of Hong Kong.

Chapter 6

Guided discussion

Problem solving 40

Solving problems or working through exercises is an important component of many subjects. Face-to-face tutorials for this type of subject usually take the form of a group of students working through problems with the help of a tutor/lecturer.

This type of academic support is well suited for the teleconference medium, because of the small group size and the interactive nature of the sessions. The aspect which may not be straightforward to transfer from the face-to-face mode is use of the visual medium. Internal classes would normally use a blackboard for writing down formulae and equations or drawing graphs and diagrams.

If a subject involves formulae, equations, diagrams or graphs, this does not imply that valuable telephone tutorials cannot take place. Indeed many successful telephone tutorials have been run for students in such visual fields as science, mathematics, engineering or economics. There are difficulties, but forethought and planning can overcome most.

This example is concerned with an elementary mathematics subject. Discussion in tutorials was centred around exercises set specifically for the tutorials. The problems in these exercises covered the range of material in a chapter and often involved synthesis of individual skills taught in the chapter. The example not only illustrates the use of guided problem solving, but also shows that mathematics is a fruitful field for group discussion and can be fun as well.

(being an abstract from the memoirs of the Duke of Gargoyle—1594 to 1537—in which he discusses an action (or, rather, inaction) at the Battle of Potzen Panz):

It was a moment of direst confusion. The Queen's own Foot and Mouth were in danger of immediate onslaught by several brigades of the Red Bladder's Saracen cavalry. In accordance with the infantry manuals, I formed the men into two squares, the total area of which was not to exceed 2,500 square yards (in order to maintain morale). In order to preserve an element of military symmetry, I further instructed my officers to ensure that the larger square should have a side length not more than 35 yards greater than that of the smaller.

The manuals assured me that the resistance of the infantry (measured in Standard Imperial Bootes) could be calculated from the sum of the side of the smaller square plus twice that of the larger. Nonetheless, I was for a while in sore confusion and knew not what to do for the best.

How could the noble Duke have employed linear programming in order to best put the Boote in? If infantry resistance had been given by the sum of the side of the larger square plus twice that of the smaller, what would then be the optimum formation?

---

extract: Armstong, P.A. (ed.) (1977) *Polymaths book C: Sets, concepts and relations.* Cheltenham: Stanley Thornes.

Own experience   41

Activity 38 mentioned the difficulty that tutors sometimes have in getting a tutorial started. Some tutors have trouble encouraging students to respond and developing a true tutorial atmosphere. One way to promote such an atmosphere is to ask students to talk about pre-set questions relating to their own experience or their current employment. Such discussion can be most easily initiated by including in the study materials activities or questions that naturally lead to exchange and communication. In particular, open-ended questions, which have no sample answers or suggested solutions, can be used very fruitfully to stimulate discussion within the tutorial group.

This example is taken from a textile and clothing course, in which all the enrolled students work in the industry and study part-time at a distance. The following activities, included in the study materials, were designed to help them to think about the effects of technological change, and to provide a starting point for tutorial discussions. Similar activities were introduced to stimulate thought and discussion of economic, social and legal/governmental change. In the original example more space is left for the students' responses.

1. Describe a recent technological change in the garment industry that has not been given in the notes.

2. Give an example of some new technology that would be suitable for your company. Could you justify its purchase in terms of the two questions posed in Section 10.2.3?

There are no sample answers to these activities, which will be discussed at a tutorial.

extract: Supervisory Studies II, Hong Kong Polytechnic.

Prescribed questions   42

Guided discussion can also be used in other ways. Academic subjects at the tertiary level are rarely black and white. Discussion of academic issues is usually seen as an integral part of a tertiary education. Teleconferencing is a means of including this important experience in external courses.

The normal attitude of philosophers to both discussion (or argument) and technology is characterised by this quotation from *The Hitch-Hikers Guide to the Galaxy.*

> We are quite definitely here as representatives of the Amalgamated Union of Philosophers, Sages, Luminaries and Other Thinking Persons, and we want this machine off, and we want if off *now!*

> Truth is quite clearly the inalienable prerogative of your working thinkers. Any bloody machine goes and actually *finds* it and we're straight out of a job aren't we? I mean what's the use of our sitting up half the night arguing that there may or may not be a God if this machine only goes and gives you his bleeding phone number the next morning? .....

> Adams 1979, p. 129.[1]

This case study concerns a group of philosophy lecturers whose antipathy towards technology was overcome by their desire to incorporate discussion among students into an external philosophy course.

---

1   Adams, D. (1979) *The hitch-hiker's guide to the galaxy.* London: Pan Books.

The main aim of the philosophy lecturers was that the students should understand the methods of philosophers and at least make steps towards successfully practising this methodology. The elements of the methodology include: reading and understanding the original works of major philosophers, analysing those works for their principal ideas, comparing and contrasting alternative ideas on the same theme and attempting a personal evaluation of the conflicting viewpoints which could be presented as a coherent written or verbal discourse. Knowledge of the principal ideas was considered important but secondary to the main aim of being able to philosophise. Students were expected to recognise that philosophy was certainly not a subject which had correct answers to every question, though many topics did have positions which would be considered sound by the majority of philosophers.

An instructional design approach was introduced which placed emphasis on the students reading original works or articles and attempting their own interpretation. Articles had to be carefully selected, especially for introductory units, as some works of philosophy can be very heavy going to the uninitiated. The students were guided through the articles by a series of comments and explanations, interspersed with questions seeking to draw out the main points of the articles. In some instances, students were asked to compare two articles with contrasting views on a topic.

In leaving more to the student there was greater encouragement and greater need for them to practice the skills of philosophers. However, there was a risk that some students were either unable to understand the readings or would misinterpret them.

This is where the teleconference came in. For internal students such problems are sorted out at the tutorials or seminars. For the external student the teleconference becomes the tutorial. Each teleconference session included a chance for the participating students to air any difficulties they had experienced. Students were asked to specify in

166

advance areas they wished to raise. However, problems were sometimes raised without prior notice, a practice which was not discouraged.

The major component of each teleconference session was a discussion on a pre-arranged topic. At intervals through the unit, topics were designated for teleconference discussion. For these topics the study guide consisted of one or more readings. Comments and interpretation from the lecturer were briefer than usual. The reading was accompanied by a series of questions. Some simply guided the students to the main points of the article while others needed a greater degree of interpretation or original thinking.

In these latter questions the students might be asked critically to analyse an argument, to compare and contrast a number of viewpoints or to form their own opinion on an issue. It was these questions which formed the agenda for the teleconference so they were highlighted in the study guide with a telephone symbol alongside. The students were expected to prepare responses to each of the designated questions for discussion in the teleconference.

The number of students involved was quite small. Some participated in the teleconference from the campus, others from one of the study centres and some from their own homes. Impressions were generally very favourable, particularly where the student lived away from one of the study centres and had experienced little or no contact with the lecturers. Several students expressed the view that philosophy was not an easy subject to study in isolation and that teleconferencing did much to relieve the lack of contact. The only non-positive comments were received from students who were behind with the unit and who felt embarrassed to participate in discussions with inadequate preparation. Eventually teleconferencing introduced an element of pacing into the courses.

The lecturers admitted to being among the least technology oriented on the campus, but soon accepted the new medium after a demonstration and became quite enthusiastic about the provision of discussion sessions for their external courses. It provided an important element of their teaching which had previously been absent for their external students. There was also a side benefit. The study guides for units incorporating teleconferencing turned out to be much smaller than the previous versions so the time needed to write and prepare them was considerably less.

This implies that the use of teleconferencing had to be designed into the course from the initial planning stages. Once the subject matter and the sequencing had been determined in the course planning sessions, sections of the course were designated for teleconferencing discussion. In selecting these sections the prime consideration was their suitability for discussion or debate; reasonably even spacing of the sessions was also desired.

The extract gives one example from the study guide. It was the first time that the writer had tried this approach which explains the note of amazement in the introduction. Not all of the questions are shown.

Introduction

Chapter 6 has not yet been written. This, I hasten to add, is quite deliberate and not the result of the writer running out of time or ideas! In a sense we want you to write Chapter 6 for yourselves. You have already read through Chapters 2–5 and, it is to be hoped, gained a good idea of Locke's political theory, and especially of his theory of political obligation. You are now to read Hume's criticism of the contract and consent theories, and Harry Beran's attempt to defend a version of the consent theory.

In the seventh week of the semester these two articles will be discussed in a tutorial. It is likely that this tutorial discussion will be held by means of one of the great wonders of our clockwork society: the conference telephone. Those of you living in different parts of the state (or indeed different parts of the world) will be able to take part in the tutorial simply by picking up your phone. (Truly we live in a Global Village!) For details of tutorial times see the section on tutorials and study schools in the Introductory Outline to this course.

Reading 6-1

Harry Beran. 'In Defence of the Consent Theory of Political Obligation and Society' *Ethics* Vol. 87, No 3 (1977), Article 3 in the Philosophy 4 Reader.

David Hume. 'Of the Original Contract' in Sir Ernest Barker's *Social Contract* , pp. 143-166

Sir Ernest Barker. *Social Contract*, pp. xi-xiv

Task

While reading these extracts attempt to answer the following questions. The tutorial discussion will be structured around those questions marked with a telephone symbol.

#-1   What are Hume's main criticisms of the contract theory of political obligation?

#-2   What are his objections to the consent theory of political obligation when that consent is understood as tacit consent?

#-3 ☎ If it is true that historically the great majority of governments have not originated from any act of consent, does this constitute a serious objection to Locke's theory of political obligation?

#-4   Does Hume believe that consent may sometimes serve as the foundation of political obligation and authority?

#-5 ☎ In the latter part of his essay Hume attempts a philosophical refutation of the 'principle of an original contract'. What is this refutation?

#-6 ☎ What is Hume's own answer to the problem of political obligation?

extract: Philosophy 4, University of Tasmania, Launceston.

Guided debate   43

Debate can be thought of as a special type of discussion in which there are two polarised views. That is, the questions under discussion tend to have two distinct camps or schools of thought. When you participate in a debate, you are expected to argue for one of these more or less fixed positions. The process of debate is not a search after the truth: it is the arguing of a point of view in which you do not necessarily have to believe.

Broad understanding can emerge as a result of trying to argue from a limited point of view. Once the nature of the "game" is accepted, the subject matter should be viewed quite clinically. In short,an arguement is usually a bad-tempered display of prejudice; a discussion is a brainstorming session in open-minded pursuit of the truth; a debate is an artificial way of exploring and testing out other peoples ideas. As such, "debate" is a High-level game entirely appropriate to the advanced study of any discipline.

The example which follows is taken from a course on *Curriculum Theory.* Debate was planned on the topic of educational objectives. The extract shows the way in which the debate was introduced in the study guide.

For and against objectives

The debate about the use of objectives:

• how to state them

- how specific or how general to make them
- who should state them
- what use are they,
  and so on,

has been with us for nearly a generation. The literature for and against is voluminous; it is often confusing because writers do not always define their terms adequately or specify the level of planning to which they are referring. Barnes tends to confuse process objectives with terminal objectives.

You need to make up your own mind about objectives. Between them, Barnes and Brady give you a good deal of information. Note that both writers tend to be biased against the use of behavioural objectives. We believe that it is valuable experience for you to learn to write specific objectives. When and whether you use them is a matter for you to decide.

What are our views?

As teachers we find it helpful in our lesson planning and in the planning of units (or series of lessons such as this one) to think very specifically about what we expect the learners to be able to do at the end of the learning. We believe this helps us to select the activities and the evaluation procedures and improves our teaching overall.

We think that specific objectives help teachers in most of their planning most of the time. There may be instances when they are not helpful, in which case they can be discarded.

Reading

Brady, *Curriculum Development in Australia* pp. 81-84

Gagné, R.M. (1972) *Behavioural Objectives? Yes!*

Kneller, G.F. (1972) *Behavioural Objectives? No!*

Combs, A.W. et al (1977) *Behaviourism and Humanism: a Synthesis*

(You will find these articles in your Reader.)

First read Brady's summary of the cases for and against specific objectives. Next, consider the debate for and against objectives between some of the 'big names' in the conflict. The three reader articles present the views of prominent writers on the subject of objectives and the related issue of behaviourism and humanism.

From this point on its up to you.

Are you for or against or do you feel happiest somewhere in the middle?

Jot down in note form your views on this subject. We will debate this issue in tutorial 2.

---

extract: Curriculum Theory, University of Tasmania, Launceston.

Individual presenter of seminar paper   **44**

A common format for seminars is to require students in the group to prepare seminar papers on different topics. Each student is then allocated a tutorial, at which they read their paper, and this is then discussed by the rest of the group.

The example is from one of the introductory subjects for a course in student guidance for school teachers. Communication strategies and group discussion methods were an inherent part of the course so it was considered desirable to have a number of seminars or colloquia. As the course was offered in Hong Kong there was less problem in bringing students together for face-to-face meetings than for some other distance education courses with more dispersed populations.

Each student was assigned a topic to present at one of the colloquia. The remaining students were all aware of the topics to be presented at each colloquium, so could prepare themselves to discuss the issues. After the colloquium the main presenter was expected to modify the paper presented and hand it in as an essay. The assessment for the introductory courses consisted of just these essays.

---

example: Social Environment and Human Behaviour, Hong Kong Polytechnic.

Pre-circulated seminar papers 45

The discussion part of the seminar format is ideal for teleconferencing. A problem for telephone tutorials is over the reading of the seminar papers. Teleconferencing is quite unsuitable for a delivery monologue of this type.

If this seminar paper format is desired for telephone tutorials it is therefore necessary to ask students to distribute copies of their papers to all other students in the group in advance of the teleconference. It is better to make the student responsible for this distribution as it eliminates double handling. The difficulty is then the short length of a semester. An appreciable time is taken by the sequence of allocating papers, the student writing the paper, distributing it to the group and they in turn reading it. At best it leaves a few weeks on the end of the semester to cram in all the papers. Asking several students to contribute papers on the one topic would cut the number of conferences needed. Running the subject over a year rather than a semester would make life easier still. For face-to-face tutorials, papers could be either distributed in advance or read at the tutorial.

An interesting use of seminar papers is provided by Laverty (1987) who used a written seminar method in a postgraduate level course. The students were first introduced to seminar methods during a summer school. Then, so that this style of teaching and learning could be continued, Laverty introduced the written seminars. He explains the basic steps of the method as follows:

1. require each member of the seminar to prepare a piece of written work—an assignment, an essay, a report, or whatever—for assessment;

2. have copies made of each of the essays and circulate these to every member of the seminar, so that each student has copies of the essays of all his/her fellow students;

3. require each student to prepare and submit critical comments on each of the essays of his/her fellow students;

4. collate these comments and have them copied and circulated, together with the lecturer's own comments, to all members of the seminar with an instruction that they examine them carefully so that they can be discussed intelligently in a teletutorial;

5. hold a teletutorial to wind up the seminar, during which the major issues raised by the essays and the comments can be discussed. In this context participants can experience some of the intellectual interaction and stimulation which face-to-face seminars are said to create, and can share the findings and insights of their fellow students.[1]

Obviously, the method is most suited to small groups, and is particularly fruitful for postgraduate work.

---

1   Laverty, J.R. (1987) The 'written seminar' method: an experiment in distance postgraduate teaching, ASPESA 8th Biennial Forum, Armidale, Australia.

Group presentation   **46**

One perennial problem with many open learning courses is that students seldom have the opportunity to work together. The benefits of meeting and working in groups are many, not the least being the social interchange and the stimulation and mutual encouragement that can result. It is also possible for students not just to meet, but to work together in groups, and to present the results of their deliberations in a variety of ways.

This extract is taken from an introductory sociology course that involves groups of students working at individual sites, who then come together in teleconferences. What follows is not a complete description, but sections of the course guide which outline the student requirements.

Lessons for Living is an exercise that helps you to think about the content of *Introductory Sociology* in a practical way by generating some policy implications of the ideas you are studying.

Specifically, here's what's required of you in preparing each *Lesson for Living*.

1. From the readings since the previous *Lesson for Living*, select some idea(s) that could have relevance to our everyday lives.

2. Prepare a statement that (a) reviews the meaning of the sociological idea(s) you have selected, (b) outlines some public policy change(s) that you think could be based on the sociological idea(s) (One way of thinking about this point is to ask yourself the following: If you were the Ruler of Canada,

how would you implement the sociological idea(s) to change the existing social arrangements?) and (c) describes the probable effects of the policy change(s) you have suggested.

This is what you need to prepare each week during the term. When it's time to utilise your preparations, here's how we'll proceed.

1. Within each site, every student will share the *Lesson for Living* that they have prepared with the others around the table. Discussion can occur among the members at each site about their peers' contributions.

2. After each person shares their preparation with others at the site, the participants will come to some consensus about which member should give their presentation to all the sites over the teleconference system.

3. Each site will then have a representative who shares a *Lesson for Living* whose strengths and weaknesses can be discussed by all of us.

The preparation of *Lessons for Living*, as well as the intra- and inter-site presentations, benefit our experience in at least the following ways.

1. Students are encouraged to be 'active' learners. Instead of just being a cerebral blotter that soaks up the content of *Introductory Sociology*, you are encouraged to participate in the construction of the course content.

2. Individually, you have a regular opportunity to think about the practical applications of the content you are studying.

3. Collectively, we benefit from discussing the correctiveness, adequacy, strengths, and weaknesses of the policy proposals you generate.

4. Finally, students get to use the teleconference equipment. Past experience suggests that more than a few students are a little shy about using the teleconference technology. If you are intimidated by the equipment, one way to get over this anxiety is to use the system so that it becomes familiar and you control it (rather than the other way around).

extract: Introductory Sociology, University of Manitoba.

Chapter 7

Case studies and projects

Analysis of presented case study   **47**

Case studies, which are simply descriptions of real-life occurrences, can be presented in a variety of ways. First, they can be presented in the course materials and discussed at tutorials. Care must be taken in the manner of presentation, especially if students are inexperienced in case study methods.

For students meeting case studies for the first time, it can be advantageous to include analysis of at least one of the cases either within the text or on cassette tape. This allows the students to appreciate the different ways that case studies can be approached, and to realise that there are no right and wrong solutions to case study problems. For further cases, the analysis can be done by the students as self-assessment, in-text or assignment questions which can be discussed at later tutorials, or the students can simply be asked to come prepared for discussion of their ideas at the next tutorial.

Another method is to have the tutor present a case study at a tutorial and act as a facilitator in the ensuing discussion. This has the disadvantage of using valuable tutorial time for presentation, but in some circumstances, for example when a case study is on film or video, this cannot be avoided. It does, though, take the pressure of having to prepare case study responses off the students. There is a tendency for students who have not prepared to miss a tutorial.

Alternatively, students can present case studies at tutorials, in much the same way as discussed in Activities 44 and 45 on Seminar Papers. This approach is particularly applicable to mature and sophisticated learners who are able to bring their wealth of practical experience to tutorial discussions.

Case studies can range in size, from short one-page descriptions, through examples which recur periodically in a subject, right on to subjects which are literally case studies in themselves. The example that we'll look at now belongs to the first category.

This case concerns a certificate level course for first level supervisors who are studying in a second language. The course includes study materials on basic supervisory practice in the clothing industry. Numerous textbooks are already available on standard supervisory techniques and theories. However, the learning materials for this subject required a Hong Kong flavour, which was not apparent in early drafts from the authors. As the students are being trained as supervisors, they need to be familiar with typical problems faced, for example, by cutting or sewing room supervisory personnel.

After some discussion on this problem, it was decided to use case studies to introduce the element of reality to the learning experience. In this way, the students could receive an appropriate mix of theory being applied to practice.

As most of the students are unused to the case study method, it was decided to introduce them to it gently. Hence the first unit has a case study that does not require analysis by the student. The analysis and application of the theory is provided in the printed material.

From the second unit on, the activities involve at least some analysis from the student. After presenting the theory, a case study is outlined, and the students are asked to apply the theory to the given problem. A typical example is found in the unit which deals with leadership. The case study involves the difficulties that a newly-appointed supervisor in a cutting room is experiencing.

Mr Tam and Mr Wu were both skilful and effective workers in the cutting room of a garment factory. When the supervisor's job became available in the cutting room, everyone knew that either Mr Tam or Mr Wu would get the job.

Mr Wu was given the supervisory position, and, as the two men were friends, Mr Tam was not too upset or disappointed. They remained friends, and Mr Wu made a special effort to spend a lot of time with Mr Tam to show that he hadn't changed, even though he had a promotion. In fact, he was even able to get Mr Tam a slight raise in pay, in recognition of his good work.

Further, because Mr Tam was good at his job, Mr Wu got him to demonstrate his cutting skills to the other workers so that they could learn from him. However, this didn't seem to work, and work levels even seemed to get worse instead of better.

Somehow, Mr Wu wasn't popular with his subordinates. He tried to talk to them to win over their friendship, and it worried him that they didn't seem to like him. The production manager was upset that work levels were so low in the cutting room, and Mr Wu wondered what he could do to improve matters.

1. What mistakes did Mr Wu make in his job as supervisor and leader in the cutting room?

2. What leadership style did he show? Give reasons for your answer.

3. What suggestions would you make to Mr Wu to improve work levels in the cutting room?

We will discuss your answers to these questions at the next tutorial.

extract: Supervisory Studies 1, Hong Kong Polytechnic.

Students developing case study

48

A meaningful use of case studies is to allow students to develop their own. Such usage can not only be beneficial to the students' professional development, it can also be of help to those involved in the case, as is exemplified by the next extract. This example is extracted from a community health subject for nurses, in which students, under fairly close guidance of an instructor, prepare a case study of a particular health problem within a small chosen community.

The focus of this practicum experience is to carry out a community study using an appropriate framework (model) such as those described in the text and course manual. The purpose is to identify an existing or potential health care problem and how the chosen community copes with it.

Guidelines

Select a community for study. This community may be a neighbourhood or specific census tracts of a larger community. This community should *not* be the larger community served by the health department, but a smaller more specifically defined area. For example in the Winnipeg area a large area such as Fort Richmond could be studied or smaller designated census tracts within Fort Richmond. The chosen community is to be negotiated with the instructor prior to any practice work.

The course instructor will provide a letter of introduction for each student which will explain the purpose of this assignment to community agencies. Ongoing consultation will also be provided to each student by the course instructor during weekly office hours. Approximately four hours of practice each week will be utilised for this learning experience and the chosen community will need to be approved before beginning the assessment.

There are several questions fundamental to a community assessment.

1. Why is it done?

2. How is it carried out?

3. Who does community assessments (i.e. whose responsibility is it)?

4. What is assessed in carrying out a community assessment? The latter depends on the purpose of the assessment and how the designated community is defined, e.g. a structural community (neighbourhood, census tract, village, etc.) or a functional community (social system, sentiment community).

5. How is the data used and by whom?

6. What are the sources of data available for a community assessment.

Information is then provided to students concerning sources of data, variables and measures to use, and how to prepare the assignments. The final part of the assignment is described as follows.

This part of the assignment is where you will integrate the collected data and make the diagnosis of the priority health problem or concern of your community. It is important to realise that some communities will be functioning at a higher level of health and therefore only a potential health problem concern will be the focus of your assessment. Rationale based on theory from the literature is to be included in this report. The following objectives will guide your presentation of relevant information.

Objectives

The student will demonstrate an analytical understanding of how a community organises itself when faced with a particular problem.

1. Indicate population, ethnic, age, and socioeconomic characteristics of the selected community.

2. Relate the demographic characteristics to the health care concerns or problems in this community.

3. Choose a specific health related problem in the selected community and define the scope and intensity of this problem (if no actual problem exists, the students should discuss a potential problem).

4. Relate the availability and usage of health care resources to the chosen health problem.

5. Describe how the selected community perceives the health problem and whether the community feels apathetic, powerless, or is activist and militant.

6. Identify the decision-making groups in the community and how they organise themselves to deal with the health problem. (These groups may be political in nature or citizen advocacy groups).

7. Evaluate the community's ability as a force to deal with the existing or potential health problems and how this affects its movement towards optimal health.

extract: Community Health Nursing, University of Manitoba.

Trigger videos 49

When television broadcasting is incorporated as a part of open learning programs there is a constrained format for delivery. Students watch the program much as they might any other television program, except some may make a recording so that they can watch it several times. However stimulating the material, it is difficult to use open circuit television as anything other than a one-way delivery mode.

Once programs are available on video cassettes, though, a great deal more flexibility can be incorporated into the way programmed material is used. There is no longer a need to view a program as an hour or half-an-hour of continuous viewing. A video cassette can be viewed in short sections with activities interspersed. Sections of programs can be viewed and re-viewed at the student's convenience.

Given this possibility, television no longer has to be seen as a medium for transmitting a message to a mass of individuals. Instead it can be used as a spur for group work.

Trigger videos are short sections of video program which are used as a stimulus for a group discussion. Usually the trigger lasts for ten to fifteen minutes at the most and they can be much shorter. A lot of images, information and ideas can be packed into a very short video segment.

Trigger videos are often visual case studies. They can be live or acted scenarios which students are expected to analyse and discuss. With a trigger video it is possible to portray a case more graphically than it can be as a description in print. The non-verbal aspects of communication can be incorporated.

The Open University of the UK has used trigger videos in its continuing education courses for practising health care professionals[1]. The courses feature periodic group meetings.

A group leader is supplied with notes on how the meetings and activities might be organised. The group leader is also supplied with a video cassette containing trigger material for many of the activities and discussion sessions.

One example of these continuing education courses is a course in nursing care for practising nurses in the field. The trigger videos included segments showing interactions between nurses and patients. Having seen the video segment the group would then be invited to discuss the segment as a visual case study of patient care. The use of a visual medium for presenting the case segment is vital because of the importance of non-verbal elements in the nurse and patient relationship.

---

1   Grant, J. (1987) Designing group work for professional updating. In Thorpe, M. and Grugeon, D. (eds.) *Open learning for adults*. Harlow, Essex: Longmans.

Projects 50

Projects inevitably need a high degree of individual advice. For open learning projects much of this takes place by one-to-one phone calls. If the interaction is confined to this individual to individual basis the students involved learn nothing of the work of their peers. They miss out on the valuable learning experiences of the research seminar, which is a part of most postgraduate study (see Activities 44 and 45).

Care has to be taken with the supervision of projects, as they have the habit of growing out of all proportion to their intended size and scope. Thus there is the danger of them occupying far more of both the tutor's and the student's time than initially planned.

The more extensive a project, the more realistic a problem students can be expected to tackle.

A final year external business degree subject is used as an example. The subject consisted of a project in which the students were expected to investigate and then propose the foundation of a viable business venture. The students then carried out steps, like drawing up contracts and arranging finance, in real life situations with co-operative lawyers and bank managers.

To monitor progress a fortnightly teleconference was held between the lecturer and the four students enrolled. Each student reported progress since the last teleconference, so each student received advice during the conference not just from the lecturer but also from their fellow students.

This way the students also learnt something from the experiences of the other students doing their projects.

At intervals during the project the students had to submit reports and other documents such as contracts and loan agreements. In each case they were required to send copies to each of their fellow students as well as to the lecturer. As the number of students was low and the distances not great there did not seem to be significant problems with this arrangement. Having documents at hand for the teleconference definitely facilitated the discussions.

example: Small Business and Entrepreneurship, University of Tasmania, Launceston.

Games   51

Games are often a part of learning, planned or otherwise. Many of today's skilled computer users started (and continue) with games that contribute to their advancement. Tutorial programs often use games to develop skills, a simple example being typing programs, many of which use arcade type games to enhance and practice keyboard usage.

Games based on computers have stolen the limelight of late, but they can be expensive to produce for limited educational purposes. However, educational games can often be produced equally well on paper or card.

Apart from management studies, academic courses are not well known for their use of games. None the less, they can play a part, depending on the subject material, the level of the course and the type of student involved.

The example shown here is a simple game, used for a higher certificate course in civil engineering for second language users of English.

Materials

Index cards approximately 13 mm x 8 mm, or, for economy, cut out your own cards from a sheet of thin white card.

Task

On one side of each card print the name or symbol of an index property, eg bulk density or γ_b. On the other side, print the definition or formula. Make up a set of cards and use them for spare-time study while travelling, etc.

A soil index-property flash card game may be played by two players. One player shows the question side of the card and the other player gives the answer. If correct, then the answering player shows a card. If not correct, the first player shows another card, and so on. Three wrong answers in a row loses the game.

extract: Geotechnology III, Hong Kong Polytechnic.

Chapter 8

Practical work

Laboratory work   52

Practical work is a feature of many distance education courses. It can be organised in a number of ways, including weekend or summer school laboratory sessions, and packages of practical work that can be completed at home.

For tutorials, practical work more usually takes the form of demonstrations of specialist equipment or experiments that cannot be easily organised elsewhere. It can also be used to supplement home experimental kits, as is shown by the next example.

This example concerns a textile technology subject which is part of a course for the training of supervisors in the clothing and textile industry. The study materials include samples of fibres, yarns, fabrics, dyes and pigments, which the students use as a basis for home experiments. Such practical activities are integrated into the study materials, being treated much the same as the self-assessment questions. The example given below is one piece of practical work which cannot be done at home as it needs an accurate balance.

At the tutorial, the students are shown how to use the balance, and they then proceed with the analysis. As the balance is needed for only part of the problem, they are able to do some of the work while waiting their turn to use the equipment.

The following activity will be done in a tutorial. This is because you are unlikely to have a balance capable of weighing the threads accurately enough. The fabric samples will be given to you at the tutorial, and you will be shown how to find the cloth weight.

Analyse the plain cotton cloth and cotton denim samples provided. The following constructional details should be found and listed:

1. ends/in and picks/in, ends/cm and picks/cm,

2. warp count,

3. weft count,

4. warp contract percentage (crimp),

5. weft contract percentage,

6. weave, and

7. cloth weight in oz/yd^2 and in g/m^2.

---

extract: Knowledge of Materials 1, Hong Kong Polytechnic.

Field trips 53

Field work can be conducted by individual open learning students as was noted in Activity 34. There are some activities which are better conducted as group activities under the supervision of a tutor. Reasons might be:

- There may be potential hazards, so a tutor needs to be present to supervise the students.

- It may be difficult for individual students to arrange access to the field site.

- The objectives for the exercise might include the development of group-work skills.

- Group field trips can develop a sense of fellowship among students enrolled for the course.

- The expertise of the tutor might be vital if students are to accomplish the planned learning tasks. The tutor is an important learning resource!

The example is taken from a course which catered for students studying in groups at a study centre with assistance from a local tutor.

Field trip: the inter-tidal area

Introduction

The inter-tidal area is the exposed sand or sand-mud area between high tide mark and low tide mark. In this area large numbers of animal live. Some wait for the tide to bring them their food, while others feed on what the tide leaves behind.

Choose a fine day when the tide is out for this exercise.

Purpose:

The purpose of this exercise is two-fold:

i)   Simply to look for and notice that a great variety of animals live in this area.

ii) To describe a few selected types and attempt to put them in the correct phyla.

Requirements:

Pencil and paper (clipped to a board so that it is firm to write on and does not fly away in the wind).

Something to dig with—a stick or small spade.

Procedure:

1.   Very briefly describe the area that you have selected to visit for your study. Include information such as: near town, near a

mangrove swamp, cut off from land by a sea wall, coral sand beach separated from land by guava scrub, pools left by tide, distance between land and low tide mark, depth of water when tide is in.

A rough map of the area will save you writing.

2   Locate about 10 different animals (look under rocks, dig in the sand, look in shallow pools, on rocks etc).

Give each animal a number, then say where it was found, what it was doing when you found it; its colour, its body shape and appendages. Suggest the phylum that you would put it into.

Note

You might find it helpful to copy out the classification of the Kingdom Animalia, pp. 227–229, to take with you.

It is not necessary to collect animals to take back home with you. Make all of your observations while in the field .

Summarise your results as follows

Where found

What doing

Colour

Size

Shape

Appendages

Classification

extract: Introductory Biology B, University of the South Pacific.